Inventing Grand Strategy
and Teaching Command

Inventing Grand Strategy and Teaching Command

The Classic Works of Alfred Thayer Mahan Reconsidered

JON TETSURO SUMIDA

THE WOODROW WILSON CENTER PRESS
Washington, D.C.

THE JOHNS HOPKINS UNIVERSITY PRESS
Baltimore and London

EDITORIAL OFFICES:
The Woodrow Wilson Center Press
One Woodrow Wilson Plaza
1300 Pennsylvania Avenue, NW
Washington, D.C. 20004-3027
Telephone 202-691-4010

ORDER FROM:
The Johns Hopkins University Press
P.O. Box 50370
Baltimore, Maryland 21211
Telephone 1-800-537-5487

2 4 6 8 9 7 5 3 1

The Library of Congress has cataloged the hardcover edition of this book as follows:

Sumida, Jon Tetsuro, 1949–
    Inventing grand strategy and teaching command : the classic works
of Alfred Thayer Mahan reconsidered / Jon Tetsuro Sumida.
        p.   cm.
    Includes bibliographical references and index.
    ISBN 0-8018-5800-3 (cloth : alk. paper)
    1. Sea-power.   2. Mahan, A. T. (Alfred Thayer), 1840–1914.
I. Title.
V25.S85   1997
359—dc21   97-26371
                                                                        CIP

    ISBN 0-8018-6340-6 (pbk.)

WOODROW WILSON
INTERNATIONAL CENTER FOR SCHOLARS
LEE H. HAMILTON, DIRECTOR

ABOUT THE CENTER

The Center is the living memorial of the United States of America to the nation's twenty-eighth president, Woodrow Wilson. Congress established the Woodrow Wilson Center in 1968 as an international institute for advanced study, "symbolizing and strengthening the fruitful relationship between the world of learning and the world of public affairs." The Center opened in 1970 under its own board of trustees.

In all its activities the Woodrow Wilson Center is a nonprofit, nonpartisan organization, supported financially by annual appropriations from the Congress, and by the contributions of foundations, corporations, and individuals. Conclusions or opinions expressed in Center publications and programs are those of the authors and speakers and do not necessarily reflect the views of the Center staff, fellows, trustees, advisory groups, or any individuals or organizations that provide financial support to the Center.

The social and psychological sources of a text are manifold—the reasons why it exists at all, and why it espouses one view of the world rather than another. But truly great works also have an internal logic that invites analysis in its own terms—as a coherent argument contained within itself by brilliance of vision and synthesis of careful construction. All the pieces fit once you grasp this central logic . . . . Great arguments have a universality (and a beauty) that transcends time—and we must not lose internal coherence as we strive to understand the social and psychological whys and wherefores.

—Stephen Jay Gould, *Time's Arrow, Time's Cycle: Myth and Metaphor in the Discovery of Geological Time*

Contents

Preface: Musical Performance, Zen Enlightenment, and
       Naval Command   xi

Acknowledgments   xix

INTRODUCTION
Resolving a Paradox   1

CHAPTER ONE
The Development of Professional Purpose, Geopolitical Vision, and
Historical Technique
    Intellectual Inheritance   9
    Education and Early Career   14
    First Article and First Book   16
    At the Naval War College   21

CHAPTER TWO
Political, Political-Economic, and Governmental Argument in the
"Influence of Sea Power" Series
    The Influence of Sea Power upon History, 1660–1783   26
    The Influence of Sea Power upon the French Revolution and Empire,
    1793–1812   32

*The Life of Nelson: The Embodiment of the Sea Power of
Great Britain* 36
Sea Power in Its Relations to the War of 1812 39

CHAPTER THREE
Strategic and Professional Argument in the "Influence of
Sea Power" Series
    Principles of Strategy 42
    Uncertainties Peculiar to the Sea 50
    Professional Implications of Uncertainty 51

CHAPTER FOUR
Strategic and Professional Argument in the Lesser Works
    Biography as Polemic 57
    Critique of Engineering and Administrative Mindsets 61
    Principles of Strategy and Their Functions 67
    Close Reasoning and Qualification 71
    Pedagogy of Command as Theology 76

CHAPTER FIVE
National, Transnational, and International Politics
    Changes of Opinion 80
    Anglo-American Naval Consortium 82
    Uncertain Prophet 92

CHAPTER SIX
The Uses of History and Theory
    Complexity, Contingency, Change, and Contradiction 99
    Naval Supremacy in the Twentieth Century 107
    Mahan, Jomini, and Clausewitz 109
    Command and History 114

Bibliography 119

Select Analytical Index to the Writings of Alfred Thayer Mahan 131

Index 163

Preface: Musical Performance, Zen Enlightenment, and Naval Command

If you study Zen, you must really study it. If you become enlightened, it must be the real enlightenment. If you once see the barbarian's real face intimately, then you have at last got "it." But when you explain what you saw, you have already fallen into relativity.

—Mumon Ekai, *Mumonkan (The Gateless Gate)*

Theory becomes infinitely more difficult as soon as it touches the realm of moral values. Architects and painters know precisely what they are about as long as they deal with material phenomena. Mechanical and optical structures are not subject to dispute. But when they come to the aesthetics of their work, when they aim at a particular effect on the mind or on the senses, the rules dissolve into nothing but vague ideas.

—Carl von Clausewitz, *On War*

Alfred Thayer Mahan (1840–1914) laid the foundations of modern naval history and strategy in his books on sea power. His main subjects were naval grand strategy and the art and science of command. The primary purpose of this book is to correct widespread and long-standing misperception of his treatment of these questions and thus facilitate a proper understanding of his thought.

Mahan's approach to naval grand strategy was relatively straightforward. It requires no further discussion here, other than to say that Mahan believed the security of a large and expanding system of international trade in the twentieth century would depend upon the creation of a transnational consortium of naval power. His handling of the art and science of command, on the other hand, was difficult, complex, and elusive. It is helpful, therefore, to achieve an introductory sense of its liminal character by means of analogy.

The performance of music, declared Thurston Dart, the famous musicologist, "is both an art and a science."[1] The art of musical performance cannot be described satisfactorily in words because even in its simplest forms it can combine complex thoughts and emotions in a manner that defies complete analysis. The science of musical performance is about mechanics, which while relatively easy to comprehend in theoretical terms, requires enormous skill and application to achieve real understanding—that is, practical mastery. Although science in the form of technical command is separate from art, it is nonetheless the medium in which the artistic impulse is communicated, amplified, and even transmogrified. In musical performance, the relationship of art and science is hypostatic and as such is an inseparable combination in which the whole may be greater than the sum of its parts. Teaching musical performance, therefore, poses three challenges: improving art, developing technique, and attending to their interaction.

In the beginning stages of learning a musical instrument or training a concert voice, instruction is mostly technical. Once basic mechanical or vocal facility is established, increasing attention is given to art. Greater concern with artistry not only adds complication in and of itself but requires the development of more refined technique to enable accurate expression of artistic intention. Every advance in the level of art, in other words, imposes new challenges of science. For this reason, technique remains a major component of instruction even at the highest levels of musical learning. The lessons given by masters to their advanced students often involve discussion of science to a far greater degree than art, not only because control over the former is the prerequisite to the exposition of the latter but also because much of the "science" portion of the teaching task can be explained in words.

---

[1] Thurston Dart, *The Interpretation of Music* (New York: Harper, 1963), 168.

The main form of artistic instruction by a master is through demonstration. The purpose of the student's reproducing the master's playing or singing is not merely to imitate but to gain a sense of the expressive nature of an act that represents authentically a human persona. Emulation of the artistic form without engagement with the source of its creation is pointless. The secondary forms of artistic instruction are two. The first is by induction, which is to say that the act of addressing science that can be applied only in the service of the highest levels of art minimally allows and maximally promotes sublime artistic expression. This amounts to an indirect approach. The second is by brief comments—critical epigrams—that illuminate a particular issue. Here the discourse, while direct, relies upon highly compressed statements to prompt an insight, not explain a concept.

The best preceptor of musical art and its relation to science is actual performance before an audience. In a concert, a musician must contend not only with unfamiliar and debilitating acoustics but with the idiosyncrasies and mistakes of colleagues and, above all, the fear of error. In addition, he or she must be capable of gauging the outer limits of expressive possibilities imposed by personal technical capability and must draw upon judgment and courage when movement to the brink or even over it may be desirable or necessary on artistic grounds. For all (or nearly all) musicians, experience—often long experience—is the principal means by which the ability to achieve creditable performance consistently, and on occasion to deliver a great one, in the face of numerous and unpredictable difficulties is created. Musical performance pedagogy reflects this elemental condition—it does not deal at length with what it cannot provide. As only part of a larger process of learning, its materials do not constitute a philosophically complete statement about musical performance. To regard them as doing so is to misunderstand both the nature of musical performance pedagogy and musical performance itself.

Naval executive officers require an artistic sensibility because in war they are confronted by problems that are difficult, complex, and unpredictable. In conflicts at sea, decisions must be made quickly in the face of incomplete or misleading information, physically arduous surroundings, manifold and unanticipatable error by subordinates, personal danger, and awareness of an awesome responsibility for the lives of others and for military outcomes. Like musicians, who must have a nearly simultaneous sense of not only their own expression but the response of the audience, with adjustments in performance made if required, naval commanders must be capable of judging situations in terms of both their own action and the reaction of their opponent and choose their course from "a flowing series of possibilities"[2] rather than a static menu of certain formulae. At the same time, the tasks of planning operations and deploying forces, though essentially technical in nature and thus largely a matter of calculation, still require prodigious mental skill and exertion to carry out effectively. The education of naval executive officers, no less than that of musical performers (and for similar reasons), must address issues of art, science, and their interaction.

Captain Stephen Roskill, the official historian of the Royal Navy during the Second World War, a participant in serious combat during that conflict, and an accomplished pianist, once devoted an entire chapter of a book on leadership to the relationship between artistic activity and operational command. "It seems to me," he observed, "that some of the greatest leaders have discovered and developed in their work a means of self-expression akin to what the painter finds in painting, the musician in the composing or playing of music, and the writer in the expression of his thoughts and feelings on paper. To such men leadership was a work of creation analogous to that of inspired painters, musicians and writers." Further on, Roskill observed that the success of Admiral of the Fleet Sir Charles Lambe—one of the Royal Navy's most brilliant officers, who served as first sea lord and was both a fine singer and keyboard instrumentalist—was attributable in large part to "his interest in the arts." To hear Lambe "playing the piano in the presence of professional musicians in the house where his flag flew as a Commander-in-Chief was an experience in the influence of artistry on leadership which can rarely have been equalled."[3]

The recent application of certain advanced technological systems to both performance-musician and naval-officer education have improved the capacity of formal instruction to engage certain important issues that were previously treated only briefly if at all. Sophisticated electronic devices that replicate aspects of performance or combat have gone beyond what could be achieved in mock concerts or naval maneuvers. But up until the late twentieth century, the older pedagogical

---

[2] Patrick O'Brian, *Master and Commander* (Philadelphia: J. B. Lippincott, 1969), 194.
[3] Captain S. W. Roskill, *The Art of Leadership* (London: Collins, 1964), 92, 102. It is perhaps significant that Jack Aubrey, the Royal Navy officer who is one of the main characters of Patrick O'Brian's remarkable series of novels about sea fighting during the Napoleonic Wars, is an enthusiastic violinist; the first book opens with an extended description of a chamber music concert. See O'Brian, *Master and Commander*, 11–14.

limits were in full force. This is crucial to understanding the work of Mahan because he was first and foremost a proponent of the idea that naval executive officer decision-making was a critical factor in war and that its quality could be enhanced through proper instruction. To serve the latter, he devoted much of his writing to the creation of a historical literature that was intended to be the basis of educating naval commanders. The main function of this body of work was teaching practice, with due recognition of the pedagogical limitations of such activity.

The formulation of theory, or the construction of a philosophically complete system of explanation, was either secondary or hostile to the accomplishment of Mahan's primary task. He wrote a great deal of historical narrative about naval operations that was based on a profound understanding of their nature and, as such, may be considered the naval pedagogical equivalent of musical demonstration. Mahan's presentation of operational principles and logistics are analogous to the discussion of musical performance technique, whose higher purpose is the induction of thinking about complexity. Critical epigrams abound. What he wrote about the contingent nature of war, the value of real experience, and his repeated explicit warnings against the dangers of mechanistic application of rules should be sufficient proof of his genuine appreciation of the artistic dimension of executive function and the inherent incompleteness of formal pedagogy. It is possible to read Mahan piecemeal and without regard for his naval professional pedagogical intentions and come to the conclusion that he was a rigid doctrinaire. That is a widely held view, but it is faulty and unjust.

The critical error made with respect to Mahan, put in more general terms, is that many students of strategic theory have mistaken the scaffolding required to construct the edifice for the building itself. They have thus not only confused a part for the whole but failed to realize that the part so engaged was supposed to be discarded after the learning task had been completed. Military leadership is responsible for both planning and the execution of plans, and while principles may guide the former, they cannot be applied mechanistically to the latter without risk of misadventure. The utility of principles with respect to the execution of planning is indirect. When used in conjunction with historical narrative and critical epigrams, principles contribute to the creation of a mental totality capable of carrying out strategic function rapidly and decisively in the face of difficulty and uncertainty. Principles, narrative, and epigrams are not the finished product; they are devices to aid the achievement of wisdom but are not the wisdom itself.

Nearly all Western religious and philosophical approaches to the problem of daily existence are concerned with the guidance or government of individual action by moral propositions. Action, in short, is subordinated to idealism, with rules or precepts constituting the instrument of influence or control. Rightness of conduct, not rapidity of response, is of paramount concern. In Zen Buddhism, however, the interposition between the individual and reality of abstract constructs, no matter how complex and sophisticated, is believed to result in distortions of perception that promote wrong action. Life, according to Zen teaching, is too variable and unpredictable to be anticipated by fixed doctrine and must be engaged as it comes with flexible judgment rather than conformation with rigid prior instruction. Zen decision-making is about decisiveness and quickness that reflect an individual's authentic sense of reality, not the holding of a certain course in accordance with markings on a moral compass constructed by others. A brief consideration of aspects of Zen Buddhism, therefore, may encourage greater comprehension of important characteristics of Mahan's thought.

Writing that does not define actual practice but serves a transitional pedagogical purpose is a tool characteristic of Zen Buddhist learning. Certain recorded statements made by a Zen master or discourse between the master and student are known as koans, which have been described as "a public document setting up a standard of judgment."[4] "What is the sound of one hand clapping?" is an example of the genre (others are provided in the epigraphs to chapters 1, 5, and 6). Koans pose intellectual problems that are not resolvable by logic alone and require strenuous mental exertion to engage. Their function, according to D. T. Suzuki, a renowned Zen scholar, is to compel the student to "go beyond the limits of intellection, and these limits can be crossed over only by exhausting oneself once for all, by using up all the psychic powers at one's command. Logic then turns into psychology, intellection into conation and intuition. What could not be solved on the plane of empirical consciousness is now transferred to the deeper recesses of the mind."[5] And once solved, "the koan is compared to a piece of brick used to knock at a gate; when the gate is opened the brick is thrown away. The koan is useful as long as the mental doors are closed, but when they are opened it may be forgotten."[6]

---

[4] D. T. Suzuki, "The Reason of Unreason: The Koan Exercise," in *Zen Buddhism: Selected Writings of D. T. Suzuki*, ed. William Barrett (Garden City, N.J.: Doubleday Anchor, 1956), 134.
[5] Ibid., 138.
[6] Ibid., 139.

Separateness of pedagogical ends and means was a fundamental aspect of Zen from its earliest existence. The Chinese Taoist sage Chuang Tzu, who lived in the fourth and third centuries B.C., presented it as follows:

> The purpose of a fish trap is to catch fish, and when the fish are caught, the trap is forgotten.
> The purpose of a rabbit snare is to catch rabbits. When the rabbits are caught, the snare is forgotten.
> The purpose of words is to convey ideas. When the ideas are grasped, the words are forgotten.
> Where can I find a man who has forgotten words? He is the one I would like to talk to.[7]

In his study of the Japanese tea ceremony, which is an art form closely related to Zen, Horst Hammitzsch, an authority on Japanese culture, observed that the "Tea Way" had "no doctrinal system of its own" because "the rules for the sequence and form of the individual actions do not provide a doctrinal framework for the Tea Way's spiritual message. And when one attempts to construct such a system according to the laws of logic, it soon becomes apparent that there is really nothing there. One merely loses sight of the vital point amid a mass of words. There *is* a vital point to the tea teaching, but it can be illustrated only through its practice and its history."[8] Hammitzsch later noted that the true "secret doctrine" had "nothing in common with the outer forms by means of which it was transmitted," these being "merely teaching aids, in the Buddhist sense, to help the disciple experience the inner meaning that cannot be expressed in words."[9]

In Japan, Zen was regarded as the basis of military as well as artistic, religious, and philosophical activity. "Since the soldiers were constantly threatened as regards their lives," Suzuki observed, "and since their swords were the only weapons that turned their fate either way to life or to death, the art of fencing developed to a wonderful degree of perfection. . . . It is not strange, then that Zen had much to do with this profession."[10] "What is most important in the art of fencing," Suzuki later argued,

---

[7] Thomas Merton, *The Way of Chuang Tzu* (New York: New Directions, 1969), 154.
[8] Horst Hammitzsch, *Zen in the Art of the Tea Ceremony* (New York: Avon, 1980), 98. Italics in the original.
[9] Ibid., 99.
[10] D. T. Suzuki, "Painting, Swordsmanship, Tea Ceremony," in *Zen Buddhism*, ed. Barrett, 289.

is to acquire a certain mental attitude known as "immovable wisdom." This wisdom is intuitively acquired after a great deal of practical training. "Immovable" does not mean to be stiff and heavy and lifeless as a rock or a piece of wood. It means the highest degree of motility with a centre which remains immovable. The mind then reaches the highest point of alacrity ready to direct its attention anywhere it is needed—to the left, to the right, to all the directions as required. When your attention is engaged and arrested by the striking sword of the enemy, you lose the first opportunity of making the next move by yourself. You tarry, you think, and while this deliberation goes on, your opponent is ready to strike you down. The thing is not to give him such a chance. You must follow the movement of the sword in the hands of the enemy, leaving your mind free to make its own counter-movement without your interfering deliberation. You move as the opponent moves, and it will result in his own defeat.[11]

Mahan's writing about the art and science of command resembles Zen in three major respects—a pedagogy that attempts to teach that which cannot be directly described in words, the absence of doctrinal ends, and a recognition of the limitations of ratiocination as the basis of action under conditions of rapid and unpredictable change.[12] Like the masters of Zen, Mahan was concerned with the creation of a disciplined yet flexible sensibility that would be capable of quick and sound judgment in spite of incomplete or misleading knowledge and risk of serious consequences in the event of error. Such a thing, he believed, required a synthesis of vigorous intelligence and strong character. The development of this practical combination of mental and moral power is the primary civic function of a liberal arts education. To engage Mahan, therefore, is not just to examine the whys and wherefores of navies; it is perforce to address more general matters—albeit within specialized contexts—that should be important to any responsible adult, and especially to his or her teachers.

---

[11] Ibid., 291.

[12] It is possible that Mahan was exposed to Zen Buddhism while stationed in Japanese waters early in his career, but there is no evidence that this was the case. For the surviving record of this period of his life, see "Diary Kept on Board the USS *Iroquois* and USS *Aroostook*, 1868–1869," in *Letters and Papers of Alfred Thayer Mahan*, 3 vols., ed. Robert Seager II and Doris D. Maguire (Annapolis, Md.: Naval Institute Press, 1975), i: 145–332. See also Captain W. D. Puleston, *Mahan: The Life and Work of Captain Alfred Thayer Mahan, U.S.N.* (New Haven, Conn.: Yale University Press, 1939), 43–5. For a Christian interpretation of Zen that resembles Mahan's religious views, see "A Christian Looks at Zen," in *Zen and the Birds of Appetite*, ed. Thomas Merton (New York: New Directions, 1968), 33–58. For Mahan's religious views, see Chapter 4.

Acknowledgments

I am indebted to professors George Baer, Daniel Baugh, Herman Belz, Arthur Eckstein, John Gaddis, John Hattendorf, James Henretta, Sir Michael Howard, Akira Iriye, Paul Kennedy, John Lampe, Herman Lebovics, George Quester, David Rosenberg, Dennis Showalter, Don Sutherland, David Syrett, David Trask, and Russell Weigley, as well as Norman Friedman, Michael Lacey, Nicholas Lambert, N. A. M. Rodger, Commander (R.N.) Jock Gardner, and Commander (R.A.N.) James Goldrick for reading various drafts and for other assistance and support. My father, Theodore Sumida, read all the drafts of the manuscript; he corrected numerous errors of style and sense, and in particular reminded me of the resemblance of certain ideas of Mahan to those of Ludwig Wittgenstein.

Most of the work on this manuscript was accomplished under the auspices of a fellowship from the Woodrow Wilson International Center for Scholars in Washington, D.C., during the 1995–6 academic year. Chris Havern, my long-time teaching assistant at the University of Maryland at College Park, served ably as my research assistant during this period. Joseph Brinley, Jr., the director of the Woodrow Wilson Center Press, was a stalwart supporter of my writing effort.

And lastly, I must express my gratitude to Arnold Jacobs and Don Smithers, both masters of music pedagogy, who were my teachers, and Emmet Larkin, my chief graduate supervisor at the University of Chicago, who taught me that when approaching a serious book, full engagement and comprehensive understanding required careful reading, a rigorous critical technique, and an educated imagination.

INTRODUCTION

Resolving a Paradox

Mahan is, and will always remain, the point of reference and departure
for any work upon "sea power."

—Paul Kennedy, *The Rise and Fall of British Naval Mastery*

The truly awesome intellectuals in our history have . . . woven varie-
gated, but firm tapestries of comprehensive coverage . . . [whose] glory
lies in their integrity as unified structures of great complexity and broad
implication. . . . What can be more destructive of our fragile [academic]
community than the mode of criticism that slices a jagged hunk out of
the tapestry, misreads and simplifies the item as a strawman in a campaign of destruction, and then tries to define the scholar by the mis-
appropriated patch?

—Stephen Jay Gould, *Eight Little Piggies*

In 1890, Alfred Thayer Mahan published a volume that has been
described as "the most powerful and influential book written by an
American in America in the nineteenth century."[1] The author was
an officer in the United States Navy, and his work, entitled *The Influ-*

---

[1] Robert Seager II, *Alfred Thayer Mahan: The Man and His Letters* (Annapolis, Md.: Naval
Institute Press, 1977), xi (hereinafter cited as *ATM*). See also Robert Bingham Downs,
Books That Changed America (London: Macmillan, 1970), 110–21; and William L. Langer,
The Diplomacy of Imperialism, 1890–1902, 2nd ed. (New York: Alfred A. Knopf, 1972), 419.

ence of Sea Power upon History, 1660–1783, was an account of European
maritime policy, naval warfare, and international politics. Virtually all
American and foreign readers viewed it as a statement of universal
truths about politics and armed conflict: that naval supremacy was the
prerequisite to national greatness and that the direction of naval operations according to certain strategic principles resulted in victory. Over
the next twenty-four years, Mahan published eighteen more books
(three of which comprised two volumes).[2] His literary popularity was
such that he was able to retire from the navy in 1896 and, until his death
in 1914, support himself and his family in modest comfort largely from
income generated by his writing.

Mahan had important things to say, but the popularity of his work
was attributable to external factors. His prolific output coincided with a
quarter century of rapid naval and maritime commercial growth at
home and abroad, during which time naval questions became more significant in world politics. Mahan caught a rising tide of public interest
in and discussion about navies, economics, and international relations.
His books, although on the whole carefully argued and finely nuanced,
were deployed as weapons in rough-and-tumble debates between proponents and opponents of naval expansion, colonialism, and aggressive
mercantilist capitalism. The intellectual substance of his publications
notwithstanding, Mahan owed much of his fortune to their utility as
polemical instruments. It was not until the flood of controversy had
ebbed that Mahan's literary remains could be admired primarily as the
founding works of modern naval history and strategy.

Esteem was one thing; understanding, another. Most readers came to
Mahan's writing with preconceptions based upon knowledge of its role
in past controversy. Reading every page of his numerous, long books required enormous effort. Mahan's range of subjects was wide, his approaches to them diverse, and his ideas complex. His output, moreover,
was spread over more than two decades, which meant that he modified
and even reversed his positions on matters great and small in the natural
course of developing his thinking. Establishing a coherent sense of the
whole, or even parts of the whole, was thus bound to be a difficult task.
Mahan's own attempt to produce a consolidated treatment of his thought
on naval operations, *Naval Strategy*, exhausted his body and depressed his
spirit. It was, in his own opinion, the worst book he ever wrote.[3]

---

[2] A list of the main editions of Mahan's books is given in the bibliography. For more detailed treatment, see *A Bibliography of the Works of Alfred Thayer Mahan*, comp. John B.
and Lynn C. Hattendorf (Newport, R.I.: Naval War College, 1986).
[3] Seager, *ATM*, 546.

The problems posed by the quantity and quality of Mahan's work were exacerbated by what was widely regarded as the unappetizing character of his writing. The French admiral Raoul Castex, for example, complained that Mahan's publications were "ponderous, rambling, ambiguous and cloudy." The naval historian, he went on to lament, "frequently repeated himself. His prose ran on and on, one tiresome affirmation incessantly succeeding another. He was a doctrinaire. He pontificated. Consequently, he is extremely difficult to read. Genuine courage is required to persevere to the end of any of his books."[4] Castex's negative views may have been in part the product of the fact that English was not his native language, but it should also be noted that Mahan's own son believed that his father's writing was "prolix" and that *The Influence of Sea Power upon History* "could have been considerably shortened to advantage."[5]

Yet Mahan's stature was such that he could not be ignored. The memory of the great influence he had wielded in his own day and the continued pertinence of certain broad applications of his thinking attracted attention. By the mid-1940s, the foundations of serious Mahan scholarship had been laid by two major biographies, a one-volume compilation of short excerpts, and two substantial critical studies of his thought.[6] This platform was extended in 1965 by a third substantial critical article; in the 1970s by the appearance of a massive three-volume edition of his surviving correspondence, which was followed by a scholarly biography by the main editor of the letters; and in the 1980s by a long critical article that was intended to replace one of the studies written in the 1940s.[7] These books and articles were utilized not only

---

[4] Quoted in Ronald H. Carpenter, *History as Rhetoric: Style, Narrative, and Persuasion* (Columbia: University of South Carolina Press, 1995), 123.
[5] Ibid.
[6] Charles Carlisle Taylor, *The Life of Admiral Mahan: Naval Philosopher* (New York: George H. Doran, 1920); Captain W. D. Puleston, *Mahan: The Life and Work of Captain Alfred Thayer Mahan* (New Haven, Conn.: Yale University Press, 1939); Allan Westcott, ed., *Mahan on Naval Warfare: Selections from the Writings of Rear Admiral Alfred T. Mahan* (Boston: Little, Brown, 1941); Margaret Tuttle Sprout, "Mahan: Evangelist of Sea Power," in *Makers of Modern Strategy: Military Thought from Machiavelli to Hitler*, ed. Edward Mead Earle (Princeton, N.J.: Princeton University Press, 1941), 415–45; and William E. Livezey, *Mahan on Sea Power*, rev. ed. (Norman: University of Oklahoma Press, 1980; first published 1947).
[7] D. M. Schurman, "The American: Alfred Thayer Mahan," in *The Education of a Navy: The Development of British Naval Strategic Thought, 1867–1914* (Chicago, Ill.: University of Chicago Press, 1965), 60–82; Robert Seager II and Doris Maguire, eds., *The Letters and Papers of Alfred Thayer Mahan*, 3 vols. (Annapolis, Md.: Naval Institute Press, 1975) (hereinafter cited as *LPATM*); Seager, *ATM*; and Philip A. Crowl, "Alfred Thayer Mahan: The Naval Historian," in *Makers of Modern Strategy from Machiavelli to the Nuclear Age*, ed. Peter Paret (Princeton, N.J.: Princeton University Press, 1986), 444–77.

as important points of reference for other writers who dealt with
Mahan, but even as substitutes for the reading of his original texts.

The views of Mahan's main ideas offered by the just-described works
did not differ from that prevalent in the author's own time: naval
supremacy was essential to any great power that desired international
preeminence, and success in war depended upon adherence to certain
strategic principles. All considered the main theme of his major histories to be the rise of British naval supremacy in the age of sail, and most
attributed the origins of Mahan's supposed insistence that command
could be reduced to a mechanistic application of principles to Antoine-
Henri Jomini (1779–1869), the Swiss military theorist.[8] These long-held
and generally accepted interpretations, however, are—if not outright
wrong—misleading to the point of error. Prejudice and incompre-
hension of Mahan's naval pedagogical sophistication, combined with
the problems posed by the length, complexity, and difficulty of his writing, led the authors of the standard monographs to misrepresent the
analytical substance of his writing. Yet such is the power of prescription
and habit that even when material by Mahan that conflicted with the
received description of the canon was occasionally noticed, inconsis-
tency was either dismissed as symptomatic of the author's lack of intellectual rigor or left unresolved.[9]

The consequences of flawed perception have been serious. Scholars,
believing the meaning of the texts to be more or less obvious, have focused on refining and elaborating understanding through the consideration of the metaphysical and physical context of his books and applying Mahan's supposed views to a variety of issues. Mahan's devout
evangelical Protestantism, some historians have argued, explained both
his advocacy of Western imperialism and his belief in historical determinism. Others have maintained that external political factors shaped
what were thought to be his fundamental ideas about strategy and policy. The balance of writing about Mahan has been devoted to the relevance of his work to past history, current events, and speculation about
the future. Such activity, although not without value, is compromised
to varying degrees by the fact that it is premised upon incorrect as-

---

[8] For the exception, see Puleston, *Mahan*, 293–8.
[9] See, for example, Herbert Rosinski, "Mahan and World War II: A Commentary from
the United States," in *The Development of Naval Thought: Essays by Herbert Rosinski*, ed. B.
Mitchell Simpson (Newport, R.I.: Naval War College, 1977), 21–2; and Bernard Semmel, *Liberalism and Naval Strategy: Ideology, Interest, and Sea Power during the Pax Britannica*. (Boston: Allen and Unwin, 1986), 94, 154, 169.

sumptions. The combination of misinterpretation, misplaced analysis, and misapplication has resulted in a striking paradox: a body of famous work that has received a great deal of study but has been misunderstood completely.

This book attempts to answer two fundamental questions about Mahan's books: did they, at any level, represent a coherent body of thought, and if so, what was its nature? In order to carry out these inquiries, the difficulties that obstructed earlier efforts to accomplish the same task have been surmounted by the following approach. The problem posed by the wide range and diversity of his subjects has been simplified by focusing on Mahan's main naval themes, which were grand strategy and the art and science of command. Grand strategy concerns the goals of national naval policy and strategy and their international context, while the art and science of command deals with the nature of operational decision-making in war. The problem of changes in Mahan's views over time has been addressed by creating two separate analytical categories: the first covers Mahan's major forms of argument, which were constants, while the second considers particular presentations of these forms, which in some cases remained the same and in other cases varied. Finally, preconceptions about Mahan have been shed and the difficulty of his writing overcome through comprehensive, repeated, and attentive reading.

The net effect of the approach just described is to make the object of inquiry the dynamics of Mahan's writing about certain important naval matters. This book, in other words, is not an exegesis of texts as such, but a descriptive analysis of Mahan's consideration of certain large phenomena. In effect, this means that his views on racism, imperialism, militarism, social Darwinism, diplomacy, and international law—which overlap those on naval matters in a number of respects but are nonetheless separate subjects—are for the most part left unexplored. Understanding a complex and sophisticated body of writing is an enormous and difficult task, one that ought to precede any systematic exploration of context or implications. The latter activities, therefore, have been reserved for another time or other hands. This volume is intended as a point of departure for further study and discussion, not as an exercise in summary or an instrument of closure.

Mahan's books on naval affairs and related matters can be divided into two groups. The core of his oeuvre is a four-part history of naval warfare from 1660 to 1815—the "Influence of Sea Power" series, after the title of the first installment. The two main subjects of these works are the relationships between naval power, economic development, and international relations (that is, naval grand strategy) and naval operations in war (in other words, the narrative building blocks for any study of the art and science of naval command). Mahan's respective utilitarian subtexts were two: the advancement of a navalist political agenda and the improvement of naval officer education. Mahan's lesser works dealt with a plethora of historical and contemporary issues. In addition to commentary on matters of the day and speculation about the future, much of this occasional output was concerned with the main subjects of the "Influence of Sea Power" series.

Mahan presented five forms of argument: political, political-economic, governmental, strategic, and professional. Mahan's political argument was that sea power had played a decisive role in the history of international relations and would continue to do so. His political-economic argument was that national prosperity—and in turn the capacity of the state to wage war—depended to a very great degree upon external trade, which required the protection of a strong navy. His governmental argument was that decision-making by the state or its primary agents in peace and war could play a decisive role. His strategic argument was that history demonstrated the existence of strategic and logistical principles that possessed a certain instructional value. And his professional argument was that in war executive officers needed to be able to make decisions quickly in the face of considerable uncertainty caused by changing conditions, incomplete or even misleading information, and fear.

Mahan's arguments were divided into two groups. Political, political-economic, and governmental arguments were the means by which he addressed his first main subject, naval grand strategy, in a manner that supported its subtext, a navalist political agenda. Strategic and professional arguments were the means by which he engaged his second main subject, the art and science of command in war, in a way that carried forward its subtext, which was advocacy of a particular form of naval officer education. In the first group, governmental argument was predicated on the proposition that decision-making by individuals—whether acting alone or collectively as the government—mattered and thus counterbalanced the determinist character of its two partner arguments. In the second group, naval professional argument, which in part emphasized the importance of judgment in war, offset a tendency toward the mechanical application of principles that was inherent in strategic argument.

In making his first group of arguments, Mahan was a political econ-
omist putting forward a clearly defined and discrete general thesis about
naval grand strategy, followed by straightforward elaboration. His intended audience was a broad one, and barring preconception or care-
lessness, the texts surrender their meaning readily. In making the second group of arguments, on the other hand, Mahan assumed the role of
a teacher of advanced practice to a body of professional specialists. The
portions of his published writing concerned with this activity, while
usable for a variety of lesser tasks, constituted the major elements of a
program of instruction in operational leadership, not the exposition of
ideas. His goal was not to give his reader command of specific propositions, but to create a total sensibility with potential for additional development through experience. Proper engagement with his material,
then, requires submission to the authority of a master, scrupulous attentiveness, and prolonged mental exertion.

The classification just given—namely that there are two types of
books and five forms of argument divided into two groups, each of
which poses different reading demands—has determined the structure
of this book. The consideration of Mahan's books is supported by a
careful examination of the military writing of his father, Dennis Hart
Mahan, who was an important influence,[10] and the younger Mahan's
surviving correspondence and early major writing. A comparison of
Alfred Thayer Mahan's views on the art of high command with those
of Jomini and Carl von Clausewitz (1780–1831), the famous early-
nineteenth-century Prussian philosopher of war, and discussion of the
connections between the works of these three men and that of Mahan's
father are provided in the concluding chapter. The large secondary literature on Mahan is surveyed and listed in the bibliography. Readers
are invited to compare the major propositions of this book with the
assumptions of earlier critical work on Mahan and to draw their own
conclusions. To assist this activity, the text has been supplemented by a
select analytical index to all of Mahan's books.

The main argument of this book is that proper engagement with
Mahan's writing can provide an understanding of his work that differs
fundamentally from previous studies, which for the most part have por-
trayed Mahan as a simplistic partisan of sea power and a proponent of

---

[10] For a contrary characterization of the relationship of the elder Mahan and his son,
which is asserted rather than argued and proved, and on the face of it almost implausible,
see Seager, *ATM*, 4.

mechanistically applied strategic principles while dismissing much of his specific strategic and political analysis as obsolete. The Mahan so regarded has been either relegated to the garbage heap of discarded scholarship or applied in corrupted form to the discussion of past history or current affairs, to questionable effect. The Mahan depicted in the following pages is the opposite of the determinist and doctrinaire; his thought and methodology, while partially outmoded, retains more instructive value than has been supposed. The new Mahan is more complex and interesting than the old. It remains to be seen whether readers exist with the mind and will to accept his guidance on what necessarily is an arduous intellectual and moral voyage into the realms of war and politics.

CHAPTER ONE

The Development of Professional Purpose, Geopolitical Vision, and Historical Technique

He made good use of his father's money.
A good son doesn't use his father's money.

—Toyo Eicho Zenji, *Zenrin Kushu*

Undoubtedly, the knowledge basic to the art of war is empirical. While, for the most part, it is derived from the nature of things, this very nature is usually revealed to us only by experience. Its application, moreover, is modified by so many conditions that its effects can never be completely established merely from the nature of the means.

—Carl von Clausewitz, *On War*

INTELLECTUAL INHERITANCE

Dennis Hart Mahan, the father of Alfred Thayer Mahan, was a distinguished instructor at the United States Military Academy at West Point. He was also the author of several important books on military engineering and warfare, as well as a standard text on civil engineering. The elder Mahan was appointed acting assistant professor of mathematics in 1821 after rising to the top of his class during his first year as a cadet. Following his graduation in 1824, he was appointed assistant professor of mathematics. From 1826 to 1830, he served as a special observer in France in order to gain information on the latest European engineering and military practices. Upon his return in July 1830, Mahan assumed the position of assistant professor of engineering. He was made acting professor of engineering in September 1830, becoming "professor of military and civil engineering, and of the science of war" in 1832, a position he held until his death in 1871.[1]

A close associate recalled that Professor Mahan as a classroom instructor possessed a "power of analysis sharpened by critical study and laborious research," which, when applied "to the consideration of a siege, a battle, or a campaign," changed "what appeared to be a complex jumble of chance events into a striking illustration of the true principles of tactics and strategy."[2] The only permanent record of Mahan's broad views on military affairs is to be found scattered through his textbooks. In his first military book, a treatise on field (i.e., temporary) fortification that was published in 1836, the elder Mahan prefaced his formal exposition of military engineering with a pedagogical manifesto. "Much that appertains to the Engineer's Art," he wrote, "is but an affair of feet and inches; facts which are the results of long usage, holding, in many instances, the important position of principles. His experience has taught him that those authors are the clearest who enter into the minutiae of their subject; and that with pupils of superior minds, a thorough knowledge of details is an invaluable aid in unravelling the difficulties, and retaining the principles of the Art; whilst, with those of limited capacities, a want of such detail leaves them with the most vague and unsatisfactory notions."[3]

The main subject of Mahan's second military book, which was published in 1847, was the tactics of troops acting in advance of the main army. In essence a technical handbook, Mahan nonetheless several times

---

[1] Thomas Everett Griess, "Dennis Hart Mahan: West Point Professor and Advocate of Military Professionalism, 1830–1871," (Ph.D. diss., Department of History, Duke University, 1969). In addition to Griess's pioneering work, see Edward Hagerman, "From Jomini to Dennis Hart Mahan: The Evolution of Trench Warfare and the American Civil War," in *Battles Lost and Won: Essays from Civil War History*, ed. John T. Hubbell (Westport, Conn.: Greenwood, 1975), 35–9; James L. Morrison, Jr., "Military Education and Strategic Thought, 1846–1861," in *Against All Enemies: Interpretations of American Military History from Colonial Times to the Present*, ed. Kenneth J. Hagan and William R. Roberts (Westport, Conn.: Greenwood, 1986), 122–3; and Russell F. Weigley, "American Strategy from Its Beginnings through the First World War," in *Makers of Modern Strategy from Machiavelli to the Nuclear Age*, ed. Peter Paret (Princeton, N.J.: Princeton University Press, 1986), 413–8.
[2] Quoted in Captain W. D. Puleston, *Mahan: The Life and Work of Captain Alfred Thayer Mahan* (New Haven, Conn.: Yale University Press, 1939), 8.
[3] D. H. Mahan, *A Complete Treatise on Field Fortification with the General Outlines of the Principles Regulating the Arrangement, the Attack, and the Defence of Permanent Works* (Westport, Conn.: Greenwood, 1968; first published 1836), vi.

made observations about the qualities required of officers faced by conditions of danger, rapid change, and uncertainty. Scouting, he noted, required "a union of courage, prudence, and discriminating observation" and thus a man capable of exercising "great boldness, caution, presence of mind and good judgment."[4] An officer in charge of skirmishers needed a "quick eye, presence of mind, and good judgment."[5] When describing the tactics of surprise and ambush, Mahan declined to give details, writing that "to trace anything more than a mere outline, as a guide in operations of this kind, which depend upon so many fortuitous circumstances, would serve little useful purpose. An active, intelligent officer, with an imagination fertile in the expedients of his profession, will seldom be at a loss as to his best course when the occasion offers; to one without these qualities, opportunities present themselves in vain."[6]

Professor Mahan's third book on matters military, first published in 1850, was a treatise on permanent fortification. In the course of describing various approaches to fortress design in this work, Mahan took the opportunity to criticize the propensity of certain engineers to codify techniques into inflexible systems. "By laying down as a principle what may be exceptionally good in practice," he wrote of one such person, "he has rather weakened his own position."[7] In his concluding pages, Mahan reiterated his distrust of system-building when dealing with a complex problem whose solution depended on particular conditions that were likely to vary widely from case to case. "Upon the chief defects and wants of the art," he observed,

> there exists but slight divergence of opinion among engineers
> generally; not so with respect to the remedy; opposite opinions
> being frequently drawn from the same class of facts, and the same
> authority frequently cited to sustain opposite views. Whilst each
> new disputant denounces systematizing and the systems of others,
> his remedy for the abuse complained of is usually a system of his

---

[4] D. H. Mahan, *An Elementary Treatise on Advanced-Guard, Out-Post, and Detachment Service of Troops, and the Manner of Posting and Handling Them in Presence of an Enemy Intended as a Supplement to the System of Tactics. Adopted for the Military Service of the United States, and especially for the Use of Officers of the Militia and Volunteers* (New Orleans, La.: Bloomfield and Steel, 1861; first published 1847), 83, 86.
[5] Ibid., 119.
[6] Ibid., 143.
[7] D. H. Mahan, *Summary of the Course of Permanent Fortification and of the Attack and Defence of Permanent Works, for the Use of the Cadets of the U.S. Military Academy* (Richmond, Va.: West and Johnston, 1863; first published 1850), 165.

own, which not infrequently offers but the *disjecta membra* of those of others. The sum of the whole matter is, that fortification is an art the component elements and principles of which are few and simple. Its efficiency consists neither in short lines of defence nor long lines of defence; nor in large or small bastions; nor in the adoption of this or that system; but in the judicious adaptation of these principles and elements to the locality to be defenced, and the purposes of the defence. In this resides the excellence of the engineer's art.[8]

Dennis Hart Mahan's fourth book on land warfare, published in 1863, was an expansion and elaboration of his second. In this work, he rejected at length and in no uncertain terms the notion that the art of command could be encompassed by any theoretical system. "In war, as in every other art based upon settled principles," he insisted, "there are exceptions to all general rules," adding that "it is in discerning these cases that the talent of the general is shown."[9] He later asked rhetorically,

How many men are there who can demonstrate the most difficult proposition of Newton's *Principia*, yet who would be puzzled to apply the most simple law of statics to some practical purpose. So is it in all the fixed sciences. In them, however, the path once entered on and there is no way of straying from it. How different in almost every military problem, except in the bare mechanism of tactics. In almost every case, the *data* on which the solution depends are wanting, or of such a character as to render it very complicated, or even indeterminate. Too often the general has only conjectures to go upon, and these based upon false premises. Even where he thinks he sees the way clearly, he knows that the rules by which he must be guided admit of many exceptions. That, whilst he is deliberating, events are succeeding each other with rapidity; that what is true now, at the next moment may have no existence, or exist in a contrary sense.[10]

---

[8] Ibid., 229. Italics in the original.
[9] D. H. Mahan, *Advanced-Guard, Out-Post, and Detachment Service of Troops with the Essential Principles of Strategy and Grand Tactics for the Use of Officers of the Militia and Volunteers* (New York: John Wiley, 1863), 207. See also 214.
[10] Ibid., 216–7. Italics in the original.

"The simple principles of the military art," he later lamented, "so simple that all can see their bearing, but . . . few, alas! can rightly apply them. . . ."[11]

Mahan senior's distaste for comprehensive theory was accompanied by an appreciation of the value of studying history: "No one can be said to have thoroughly mastered his art who has neglected to make himself conversant with its early history; nor, indeed, can any tolerably clear elementary notions, even, be formed of an art, beyond those furnished by the mere technical language, without some historical knowledge of its rise and progress; for this alone can give to the mind those means of comparison, without which everything has to be painfully created anew, to reach perfection only after many cycles of misdirected mental toil."[12] "It is in military history," he later maintained with greater specificity, "that we are to look for the source of all military science. In it we shall find those exemplifications of failure and success by which alone the truth and value of the rules of strategy can be tested. Geometrical diagrams may assist in fixing the attention, and aiding by the eye the reasoning faculties; but experience alone can fully satisfy the judgment, as to the correctness of its decisions, in problems of so mixed a character, into which so many heterogeneous elements enter."[13]

Dennis Hart Mahan encouraged all his children to read books and to develop their minds.[14] The senior Mahan lived until his first son's thirty-first year, and the latter recorded several instances of their conversations about serious subjects in his memoirs.[15] It is, therefore, highly likely that there was a good deal of conversation between the two about military issues, especially during the Civil War, a conflict in which nearly all the senior commanders on both sides had been known to Professor Mahan as students.[16] Alfred Thayer Mahan did not acknowledge his father as the source of his own views on discipline, the contingent nature of war, and the uses of principles and history, but the

---

[11] Ibid., 235.
[12] Ibid., 7.
[13] Ibid., 216–8. For Mahan's advocacy of military history properly taught, but his opposition to its inclusion in the curriculum when presented as little more than chronology, see Griess, "Dennis Hart Mahan," 230–9, 244–8.
[14] Puleston, *Mahan*, 12–3.
[15] Captain A. T. Mahan, *From Sail to Steam: Recollections of Naval Life* (New York: Harper and Brothers, 1907), 91–2, 154–5.
[16] Weigley, "American Strategy," 415. The notable exception was Robert E. Lee, who was not a student of Mahan's but who served as commandant of West Point from 1852 to 1855.

consonance of the thinking of father and son on these matters is striking. Given the nature of the relationship between the two men, the conclusion that the influence of the elder Mahan upon the younger was considerable seems inescapable.

EDUCATION AND EARLY CAREER

Alfred Thayer Mahan was born in 1840. In 1856, he entered the United States Naval Academy as a cadet and in 1859 graduated near the top of his class in spite of less-than-full engagement with his studies. As an upperclassman, he attempted to raise the midshipmen's standards of discipline, which were lower than those at West Point and not those that his upbringing had accustomed him to accept as befitting a military organization. Mahan's efforts were resisted tenaciously, however; they caused him to be ostracized by many of his peers and were ultimately unsuccessful. His quixotic campaign was, among other things, an early manifestation of what would be a life-long concern for discipline, a reflection of an exalted view of the status of executive command. It may be significant that his father supported and encouraged his son during this difficult period.[17]

At the Naval Academy, Mahan was trained in sailing ships and in using their equipment. He then went on to serve at sea during the Civil War, which in many ways resembled a preindustrial maritime conflict because of the primitive state of industrial matériel. After the war, Mahan was posted to ships and land establishments that retained much of the character of an earlier age. His knowledge of naval warfare as it was before his time was by no means perfect. For example, he seems— on the basis of what was *not* said in his later writing—to have been ignorant of certain important late-eighteenth-century innovations in ordnance and gunnery, signaling, and hull maintenance.[18] But in spite of

---

[17] Puleston, *Mahan*, 22–3; Robert Seager II, *Alfred Thayer Mahan: The Man and His Letters* (Annapolis, Md.: Naval Institute Press, 1977), 24–31 (hereinafter cited as *ATM*). For what was in certain respects Dennis Hart Mahan's similar experience at West Point in 1834, see Griess, "Dennis Hart Mahan," 153–5. For the unruly character of midshipmen at the Naval Academy in Mahan's day, see Charles Todorich, *The Spirited Years: A History of the Antebellum Naval Academy* (Annapolis, Md.: Naval Institute Press, 1984), chaps. 5 and 6.
[18] Brian Lavery, *The Arming and Fitting of English Ships of War, 1600–1815* (Annapolis, Md.: Naval Institute Press, 1987), 62–5, 104–9, 123–4, 143; and Brian Lavery, *Nelson's Navy: The Ships, Men, and Organisation, 1793–1815* (Annapolis, Md.: Naval Institute Press, 1989), 82–4, 260–4.

such shortcomings, his involvement with both executive command and administration under archaic conditions provided him with virtually a practitioner's understanding of pre-industrial navies as institutions, with the added advantage of hindsight.[19]

After the Civil War, Mahan was alarmed by the rising status of naval officers who served in administrative or other supporting positions; he believed their pretensions had begun to interfere with the proper exercise of executive authority.[20] "It is a singular fact that in a simply [*sic*] military organization like the Navy," he wrote on 27 January 1876 to Samuel A. Ashe, a former classmate at the Naval Academy who had left before graduating,

> the military branch has been gradually losing power and influence, and after due deduction from their complaints, on the score of the human tendency to complain, [there] can be no doubt they have been subjected to almost degradation of late years. All is so changed since you knew us familiarly that you will be surprised to learn that so much rank has been given to the staff as they are now called, i.e. doctors paymaster & engineers, that it is difficult to find officers of those corps who being sent on board ship are not senior to the first lieutenant (now executive officer). . . . For after all the Navy exists simply as a military body for fighting purposes, and as for the incidental duties of sea going, surveying, holding quasi diplomatic relations in certain cases—protecting commerce & American interests; in all these it is the line officer who acts, thinks, is responsible, and the other bodies are merely adjuncts, necessary adjuncts as is the ship itself—but plainly and simply and essentially subordinate.[21]

The next month, Mahan complained that the control just given to naval administrative officers over the management of ship construction and repairs constituted a serious breach of the authority of naval executive officers. The "power of the line officers in the Navy Yards has

---

[19] Puleston, *Mahan*, 96–7.
[20] Seager, *ATM*, 105–10. For the line-versus-staff controversy, see Rear Admiral Albert Gleaves, *Life and Letters of Rear Admiral Stephen B. Luce* (New York: G. P. Putnam's Sons, 1925), 336–48.
[21] Mahan to Samuel A. Ashe, 27 January 1876, in *The Letters and Papers of Alfred Thayer Mahan*, ed. Robert Seager II and Doris Maguire, 3 vols. (Annapolis, Md.: Naval Institute Press, 1975) (hereinafter cited as *LPATM*), i: 440–1.

been abolished to all intents and purposes," he wrote to Ashe, "and the chief power given to constructors. If the country wants the Navy Yards purely administered—it is necessary to put into the hands of the Commandants unchecked control over employment and dismissal—and give him subordinates who shall have the power of overlooking and controlling the workmen."[22]

Mahan was incensed in particular by the political corruption of dockyard administration. In 1876, his testimony before a congressional committee about this problem prompted his superiors to cast him into semi-retirement, which resulted in a sharp reduction in income. Although these circumstances did not last long, they transformed his irritation over violations of public probity into a resentment that was fueled by a deep sense of personal grievance.[23]

FIRST ARTICLE AND FIRST BOOK

In 1879, while serving as head of the Ordnance Department at the Naval Academy, Mahan produced his first publication, an article that appeared in the *United States Naval Institute Proceedings* after winning third prize in an essay contest whose theme was "Naval Education for Officers and Men." In this piece, Mahan argued that above all, the line officers of the navy needed moral power, which to him meant, among other things, "fearlessness in responsibility and in danger," "self-reliance," and "promptitude in action." The existing emphasis on science and engineering, he believed, tended "to promote caution unduly; to substitute calculation for judgment; to create trust in formulas rather than in one's self."[24] Later on, Mahan insisted that

> the organizing and disciplining of the crew, the management under all circumstances of the great machine which a ship is, call for a very high order of character, whether natural or acquired; capacity for governing men, for dealing with conflicting tempers and interests jarring in a most artificial mode of life;

---

[22] Mahan to Samuel A. Ashe, 1 February 1876, *LPATM*, i: 443.
[23] Seager, *ATM*, 114–5.
[24] Commander A. T. Mahan, "Naval Education," *United States Naval Institute Proceedings* 5 (1879): 347. For the resemblance of these views to those of his father, see Griess, "Dennis Hart Mahan," 114, 182.

self-possession and habit of command in danger, in sudden emergencies, in the tumult and probable horrors of a modern naval
action; sound judgment which can take risks calmly, yet risk no
more than is absolutely necessary, sagacity to divine the probable
movements of an enemy, to provide against future wants, to avoid
or compel action as may be wished; moral courage, to be shown
in fearlessness of responsibility, in readiness to either act or not
act, regardless of censure whether from above or below; quickness of eye and mind, the intuitive perception of danger or
advantage, the ready instinct which seizes the proper means in
either case: all these are faculties not born in every man, not perfected in any man save by the long training of habit—a fact to
which the early history of all naval wars bears witness.[25]

Mahan was angered by the degree to which the development of executive ability in war seemed to have been subordinated to the requirements of producing a level of scientific literacy that was far beyond that
needed by a naval officer:

I confess to a feeling of mingled impatience and bitterness
when I hear the noble duties and requirements of a naval officer's
career ignored, and an attempt made to substitute for them the
wholly different aims and faculties of the servant of science. The
comparatively small scale on which those duties are now performed, the fancied impossibility of a great war, the pitiful condition of efficiency into which the material of the navy has been
allowed to fall, have all helped to blind our eyes to the magnifi-
cence of the war seaman's career. At the same time science has
been, and still is, achieving her magnificent conquests; and men,
as always, in the presence of the achievements of the moment
forget the triumphs of the past. No wonder the line officers of
the navy are themselves carried away by an amazed humility
which falsely dwarfs their own profession.[26]

Mahan appears to have been satisfied with the existing standard of
history instruction, which was more or less subsumed by course work in

---

[25] Ibid., 353.
[26] Ibid., 349.

English, naval tactics, and foreign languages.[27] "Although none of these are dignified by the name of science," Mahan observed,

> few will find fault with the extent to which they are now carried at Annapolis. About Naval Tactics I shall here say nothing. If I be asked, in my own words, how the English studies or the acquirements of Foreign Languages help a man to handle and fight his ship, I will reply that a taste for these two pursuits tends to give breadth of thought and loftiness of spirit; the English directly, the Foreign Languages by opening their literature. The ennobling effect of such pursuits upon the sentiment and intellect of the seaman helps, I think, to develop a generous pride, a devotion to lofty ideals, which cannot fail to have a beneficial effect upon a profession which possesses, and in its past history has illustrated in a high degree, many of the elements of heroism and grandeur. The necessarily materialistic character of mechanical science tends rather to narrowness and low ideals.[28]

In addition to justifying the continuation of nonscientific coursework, Mahan called for the elimination of physics and chemistry, and some mathematics, to allow time for the study of drawing, modern languages, mechanics, and steam engineering.[29] His recommendations for concomitant changes in the structure of the officer corps were no less radical. The navy as it stood seemed to be committed to the notion that all naval officers should possess substantial scientific ability. Mahan's view was that executive capacity was more important and that the bulk of the navy's officer requirements should be fulfilled by men whose education had been designed to promote it. Scientific and mechanical expertise, while essential to the navy, was to be left in the hands of a minority who had displayed an aptitude for the material aspect of naval affairs: "Devotion to science and the production of the instruments of warfare, from the ship itself downwards, should be the portion of certain, relatively small, classes of specialists."[30] The segregation of technical and executive function was essential, Mahan believed, because "the attempt

---

[27] For the similarity of Mahan's position on the teaching of history with that held by his father, see Griess, "Dennis Hart Mahan," 232–4, 239, 242, 244–8.
[28] Ibid., 352.
[29] Ibid., 358–9
[30] Ibid., 352.

to combine the two has upon the whole been a failure, except where it has succeeded in reducing both to mediocrity in the individual."[31]

Over the next several years, Mahan was in no position to give much effect to his views. On the other hand, domestic requirements and a literary opportunity prompted him to develop the skills of a historian. In the early 1880s, he provided his elder daughter with a course of instruction in the political history of England and France. To carry this out, Mahan produced notebooks that were based upon his reading of standard general histories and sought to explain complex subjects by means of skillful selection and condensation. During the spring of 1882, he wrote *The Gulf and Inland Waters*, the concluding volume in a three-part series on the naval side of the Civil War. Mahan had served in this theater during the hostilities, read the voluminous official reports of operations from both sides, and corresponded with numerous participants. Mahan's approach to operational history was critical and analytical, based upon both direct experience and scholarly research.[32]

In this work, Mahan touched upon several themes that would be developed in his later work. In the first place, he noted the dependence of the South upon external trade. The purpose of the Union blockade, he maintained, "was to close every inlet by which the products of the South could find their way to markets of the world, and to shut out the material, not only of war, but essential to the peaceful life of a people, which the Southern States were ill-qualified by their previous pursuits to produce."[33] Mahan also made a point of describing Union unpreparedness and the importance of finance: "The construction and equipment of the fleet was seriously delayed by the lack of money, and the general confusion incident to the vast extent of military and naval preparations suddenly undertaken by a nation having a very small body of trained officers, and accustomed to raise and expend comparatively insignificant amounts of money."[34]

Mahan praised then–Flag Officer David Glasgow Farragut's swift capture of New Orleans in 1862 on the highest political as well as military grounds. "There is strong reason to believe," he argued, "that the fall of New Orleans nipped the purpose of the French emperor, who had held out hopes of recognizing the Confederacy and even of declar-

---

[31] Ibid., 353. Seager's representation of Mahan's views in this essay is highly misleading. See Seager, *ATM*, 120.
[32] Puleston, *Mahan*, 62–5; and Seager, *ATM*, 135–7.
[33] A. T. Mahan, *The Gulf and Inland Waters* (New York: Charles Scribner's Sons, 1883), 4.
[34] Ibid., 16. For the importance of maintenance and logistics, see also 91.

ing that he would not respect the blockade if the city held out."[35] This observation, as well as his previously noted remarks about the goals of the Union blockade, suggest that Mahan recognized the relationship between war operations on the one hand, and economics and politics on the other, well before he read about such matters in the works of Jomini in the late 1880s. The foundations, in other words, of his later work lay further back in his past than suggested by certain reminiscences in his memoirs.[36]

Mahan took a number of opportunities to advance his views about the qualities of executive leadership that were required in war. Much of his case was put in the form of negative assessments. "There can be no denying the dash and spirit with which this attack was made," Mahan wrote of a Confederate sortie but dismissed it as an act of limited worth performed by an "irregular and undisciplined force."[37] The generally poor performance of the Confederate riverine units was attributed to the fact that "there was no organization, no discipline, and little or no drill of the crews."[38] Occasions of incompetence on his own side were also marked. The success of a Confederate surprise attack was made certain when a Union officer "unfortunately waited for orders to act."[39] The unnecessary loss of a Union gunboat was given as "another instance of how lack of heed in going into action is apt to be followed by a precipitate withdrawal from it and unnecessary disaster."[40]

Mahan also presented his case in positive terms by describing instances in which calculation and a willingness to accept risks were mated to achieve success. He praised Flag Officer Andrew Hall Foote, the commander of the Union Navy's small flotilla on the Mississippi River, for first resisting strong and unreasonable calls by the army and public opinion for offensive action and then launching a daring attack when conditions changed, thus "showing that no lack of power to assume responsibility had deterred him before."[41] Mahan observed that the bold entry into the harbor at Mobile in 1864 in the face of mines had been based on now–Rear Admiral Farragut's calculation that the favor of a flood tide would render the mines ineffective. The admiral,

---

[35] Ibid., 86.
[36] Mahan, *From Sail to Steam*, 283. On this matter, see also Puleston, *Mahan*, 61.
[37] Mahan, *Gulf and Inland Waters*, 45.
[38] Ibid., 84n.
[39] Ibid., 101.
[40] Ibid., 128.
[41] Ibid., 37.

Mahan pointed out, had not gone "heedlessly into action" but had "reckoned on torpedoes [mines] and counted the cost."[42] Mahan also told the story of the Union captain at Mobile who, knowing that "the bottom was a soft ooze," ignored warnings that the water was too shallow in order to carry out his orders to advance and insisted that the man measuring the depths be called in because "he is only intimidating me with his soundings."[43]

AT THE NAVAL WAR COLLEGE

In 1886, Mahan joined the faculty of the newly established Naval War College. While serving as its president (1886–9), and in this capacity finding it necessary to resist efforts to close it, he had occasion to again put forward his views on the need to give the development of efficient executive officers precedence over that of officer technicians. "The present predominant tendency of the naval mind," he wrote on 13 October 1888, "as evidenced by the literature in which it finds expression and the work on which its practical energies are expended, is toward mechanical progress and development of material, rather than toward the study of the military movements which that material is to subserve."[44] "I suppose we have all admitted to ourselves by this time," Mahan explained on 22 November 1888, "that we can no longer hope to be abreast of the advance in all matters of professional interest. The complex development of the present day has reconciled us to specialties, and to bring ourselves non-specialists in some, perhaps in many, of the necessary factors that make up a modern war-ship. If there be, however, any one branch in which we should have clear views, a wide and deep knowledge, not only of the truths, but of the reasons and arguments by which those truths are established, it is the conduct of war, or art of war. . . . "[45]

By now, Mahan had come to the conclusion that the "deep knowledge" and "truths" would have to come from the study of history. While his own upbringing and recent experience would have predisposed him to favor such a course, he also had had an immediate and unhappy encounter with an alternative approach. From October 1885

---

[42] Ibid., 232.
[43] Ibid., 239. For the notice taken of Mahan's special pleading of the cause of the executive officer, see Seager, *ATM*, 136.
[44] Mahan to John G. Walker, 13 October 1888, *LPATM*, i: 661.
[45] Mahan to Charles R. Miles, 22 November 1888, *LPATM*, i: 667.

to May 1886, Mahan had labored over lectures devoted to steam battle-fleet tactics, in which he attempted, with little enthusiasm, to produce a command primer based upon a comprehensive and systematic consideration of modern technical capabilities.[46] In his examination of torpedo warfare, he found an opportunity to comment on the importance of leadership, noting that "the whole history of warfare proves . . . that all desperate enterprises which require not only courage, but skill used with coolness are peculiarly open to failure."[47] But otherwise, Mahan's piece was concerned almost exclusively with matériel.

Captain Stephen Luce (1827–1916), the founder and president of the War College, found the written-out lectures no more than "in the main, satisfactory," and the manuscript lapsed into unpublished obscurity.[48] While working on this project, Mahan confessed to Ashe on 2 February 1886 that

> to excogitate a system of my own, on wholly a priori grounds would be comparatively simple and I believe wholly useless. We are already deluged with speculations and arguments as to future naval warfare—more or less plausible and well considered; but I don't see any use in my adding to that clack. I want if I can to wrest something out of the old wooden sides and 24 pounder that will throw some light on the combinations to be used with iron-clads, rifled guns and torpedoes; and to raise the profession in the eyes of its members by a clearer comprehension of the great part it has played in the world than I myself have hitherto had.[49]

Reflection over his reading of history, moreover, had by this time caused Mahan to relate the question of naval power to larger political and economic issues. In 1884, while in command of a warship off the coast of Peru, he had read the German historian Theodor Mommsen's *The History of Rome* by way of preliminary preparation for his forthcoming duties as an instructor at the Naval War College. Mommsen's account of the Carthaginian Wars prompted Mahan to consider the extent to which

---

[46] A. T. Mahan, "Fleet Battle Tactics," lecture (1886), Record Group 14, Naval War College Archives, Newport, R.I. (courtesy of Professor John Hattendorf). For the use of portions of this manuscript in *Naval Strategy* (1911), see Seager, *ATM*, 637.
[47] Mahan, "Fleet Battle Tactics," 3.
[48] Quoted in Seager, *ATM*, 164. For a slightly different text, see John D. Hayes and John B. Hattendorf, eds., *The Writings of Stephen B. Luce* (Newport, R.I.: Naval War College, 1975), 53.
[49] Mahan to Samuel A. Ashe, 2 February 1886, *LPATM*, i: 625.

Hannibal's land campaigns had been crippled by his inability to transport his army by sea or to otherwise maintain over-water communications with Carthage because of Roman naval superiority. The outcome of the great struggle, he concluded, was decided in Rome's favor by her use of naval force, the fighting of great battles on land notwithstanding. Mahan then proposed that the results of the wars between Britain and France in the late seventeenth and eighteenth centuries could be explained similarly. Lectures devoted to this later period, he realized, would illustrate what he regarded as an elemental truth—namely, that sea power determined the course of history and thus the prosperity of nations.

For several reasons, this concept was a matter of major practical significance to Mahan. In 1884 and 1885, his experience off the coast of Central and South America during periods of civil unrest had undermined his anti-imperialist sentiments and fostered a greater appreciation of the need for the United States to develop substantial naval power as a means of keeping the peace in the Western Hemisphere. During these same years, moreover, the vicissitudes that had attended his command of a worn-out and undermanned vessel that was made of wood, powered by sails as well as steam, armed with antiquated guns, and supplied by an inadequate number of coaling stations had both obstructed the carrying out of orders and offended his professional pride. Thus by the time he took his place at the War College in 1886, Mahan was strongly supportive of efforts to modernize and expand the navy.

At the War College, Mahan's intellectual inheritance from his father, long-standing concern with what he considered was the unsatisfactory condition of naval executive-officer education and status, and recently acquired imperialist and naval expansionist opinions were mixed together with systematic reading of Jomini.[50] Jomini's influence on Mahan was important but limited. Luce may at this time have believed that all operations of war should be governed by the application of fundamental principles in what he believed was the scientific—that is to say, mechanistic—manner of the Swiss theorist,[51] but Mahan's views on

---

[50] Mahan, *From Sail to Steam*, 283; and Seager, *ATM*, 166–9.
[51] Stephen Luce, "England and France on the Sea," *The Critic* 22 (14 January 1893), 17, reprinted in *The Writings of Stephen B. Luce*, ed. John D. Hayes and John B. Hattendorf (Newport, R.I.: Naval War College Press, 1975), 105, quoted partially in Seager, *ATM*, 164. But a much more nuanced position is given in Stephen Luce, "Stonewall Jackson and the American Civil War," *The Critic* 34 (January 1899), in *The Writings of Stephen B. Luce*, 107. The discussion of strategy and command in the 1899 article is practically identical to that of the two Mahans, with an emphasis on art and the necessity of taking responsibility in order to act decisively.

the nature of strategic principles and their utility followed that of his father, who had placed greater emphasis on the artistic attributes of effective command. What Jomini gave Mahan was the conception of decisive battle as the resolver of strategic difficulty, particular principles such as concentration of force, and a model of presenting analysis in the form of narrative accompanied by critical commentary.[52]

The combination of ideas passed to him from his father, professional dissatisfaction, interest in contemporary international politics, and study of Napoleonic warfare as presented by Jomini produced in Mahan a powerful intellectual reaction that generated a broad and complex conception of naval history in the preindustrial era and a connection of that conception to current national affairs. Following the completion of his lectures on steam battle tactics in the spring of 1886, Mahan turned to the preparation of a separate collection of lectures on naval history in the age of sail. A broad draft outline was completed by the end of the summer. This served as the basis of lectures given at the War College in 1886, 1887, and 1888. While teaching, Mahan revised and refined his text. Finishing the task in the fall of 1888, he began his search for a publisher. After several refusals and further revisions, the manuscript was accepted by Little, Brown, and Company of Boston and appeared in May 1890 as *The Influence of Sea Power upon History, 1660–1783*.

Prior to publication, Mahan probably believed that the importance of the book lay in its contribution to the improvement of naval professionalism. As has been explained, he was convinced that constant and rapid mechanical innovation had upset planning and education to the detriment of command confidence and authority. He feared the consequences of a navy led by indecisive men, bred by bureaucratic routine— or worse, subservience to corrupt civilian officialdom—to follow rules or act politically. Referring to his forthcoming book, he wrote in May 1890 to W. H. Henderson, an English friend and critic, that he had "great hopes that it will in a short time make some substantial contribution to naval thought, and perhaps persuade our people that naval matériel is not all the battle; that first-rate men in second-rate ships are better than second-rate men in first-rate ships."[53]

In the spring of 1889, however, the passage of legislation in Britain that provided for the construction of numerous battleships of unprece-

---

[52] For a sound and detailed discussion of the specifics of Mahan's reading of Jomini in the 1880s, see Seager, *ATM*, 164–73. See also Mahan, *From Sail to Steam*, 283.
[53] Mahan to William H. Henderson, 5 May 1890, *LPATM*, ii: 9.

dented size and power, as well as many cruisers, had prompted Luce to publish a call for a similar program in the United States. Luce's article was followed by the creation of a "Policy Board" by the secretary of the navy that was charged with the task of investigating questions related to future naval construction.[54] The public controversy raised by these events was probably the cause of Mahan's hurriedly adding in the fall of 1889, at the suggestion of his publisher, an extended introductory chapter, entitled "Elements of Sea Power."[55] This new section was primarily devoted to propositions about the importance of naval strength, its relationship to national development, and the relevance of this relationship to American circumstances. To be sure, these issues were handled in the main text, but the form and content of the addition and its placement at the beginning had the effect of shifting the emphasis of the entire volume to favor the geopolitical theme over the operational. It was this material that captured the attention of critics and the reading public, and to a very great degree, has defined the perception of Mahan's writing ever since.

---

[54] Benjamin Franklin Cooling, *Benjamin Franklin Tracy: Father of the Modern American Fighting Navy* (Hamden, Conn.: Archon, 1973), 72–4.
[55] Seager, *ATM*, 205.

CHAPTER TWO

Political, Political-Economic, and Governmental Argument in the "Influence of Sea Power" Series

If you want to get hold of what it looks like, do not be anti- or pro-anything.

—Zen proverb

. . . Place fact and description before theory.

—Stephen Jay Gould, *Wonderful Life*

THE INFLUENCE OF SEA POWER UPON HISTORY, *1660–1783*

The opening of *The Influence of Sea Power upon History, 1660–1783* was devoted mainly to the presentation of Mahan's political, political-economic, and governmental arguments, which were interrelated. Mahan considered these three to be "strategical" according to a broad definition of naval strategy that included national maritime and naval policy in peace, yet distinct from questions related exclusively to war operations, which define the domain of strategic argument in the present work.[1]

---

[1] Alfred Thayer Mahan, *The Influence of Sea Power upon History, 1660–1783* (Boston: Little, Brown, 1890), 89.

Mahan stated his political argument in his preface: maritime affairs had had a large and even decisive effect "upon the course of history and the prosperity of nations."[2] This position was softened by a degree of qualification. While Mahan insisted that sea power had been an "immense determining" force, he conceded that "it would be absurd to claim for it an exclusive influence."[3] He maintained, in addition, that "sea history" was "but one factor in that general advance and decay of nations which is called their history" and that "if sight be lost of the other factors to which it is so closely related, a distorted view, either exaggerated or the reverse, of its importance will be formed."[4]

Mahan's political-economic argument was founded upon the economic proposition that "travel and traffic by water have always been easier and cheaper than by land."[5] Although he recognized that railroads had largely displaced water transport for internal economic activity in his own time, he maintained that ships still constituted the primary form of carriage for external trade and would remain so in the future.[6] Mahan's political-economic argument proper had three aspects. First, maritime economics—that is, production, shipping, and colonies—was the key to national prosperity and had been a prime motivator of the policies of states bordering on the sea.[7] Second, that throughout history, the possession of naval supremacy was essential to the protection of national interests related to production, shipping, and colonies, and therefore had been a factor of critical importance in conflicts between great states.[8] And third, a country's capacity to develop sea power was affected by six "principal conditions": geographical position, physical conformation (which included natural resources and climate), extent of territory, population size, national culture, and political structure.[9]

---

[2] Ibid., xiii.

[3] Ibid., 21.

[4] Ibid., 90. See also 225–6. For Mahan's admission that the treatment of general history would be "intentionally slight," see vi.

[5] Ibid., 25.

[6] Ibid., 26. These economic propositions will not be discussed again in the present work, and for this reason mention is made here of the fact that they were repeated later in his lesser works, for which see A. T. Mahan, "The Problem of Asia" (I, II), *Harper's New Monthly Magazine*, (March and May 1900), reprinted in A. T. Mahan, *The Problem of Asia and Its Effect upon International Policies* (Boston: Little, Brown, 1900), 38, 125–6; and A. T. Mahan, "The Hague Conference: The Question of Immunity for Belligerent Merchant Shipping," *National Review* (July 1907), reprinted in Captain A. T. Mahan, *Some Neglected Aspects of War* (Boston: Little, Brown, 1907), 176–7.

[7] Mahan, *Influence of Sea Power upon History*, 1, 28.

[8] Ibid., 1.

[9] Ibid., 29–89.

These ideas were not original. Mahan for the most part had simply restated thoughts that had been put forward by others.[10] That there had been much previous independent musing upon the sources and significance of naval power, however, meant Mahan's first major book fell upon a reading public well-primed to accept a coherent presentation of certain large issues. And it was the treatment of these political-economic questions that seems to have been the focus of contemporary reviewers and subsequent commentators.[11] The six "principal conditions" in particular have been characterized as the heart of Mahan's political-economic exposition.[12] But Mahan intended this material to serve primarily as a foil for his governmental argument, which was about the appropriate role of state action with respect to naval development.

Mahan conceded that a country's capacity to develop sea power was largely determined by the six principal conditions. But he also insisted that "the wise or unwise action of individual men has at certain periods had a great modifying influence upon the growth of sea power in the broad sense, which includes not only the military strength afloat, that rules the sea or any part of it by force of arms, but also the peaceful commerce and shipping from which alone a military fleet naturally and healthfully springs, and on which it securely rests."[13] Mahan was convinced that the history of the great Anglo-French conflicts of the late seventeenth and eighteenth centuries provided ample material to illustrate this contention, which was meant to encourage his own government to pursue a much more vigorous naval and maritime policy. While he cautioned his readers that he was not "asserting a narrow parallelism between the case of the United States and either [Britain or France],"[14] he left little doubt that his chief interest was in the behavior of France, in spite of the attention that he paid to Britain.

Mahan attributed Britain's rise in the eighteenth century to "her government using the tremendous weapon of her sea power,—the reward

---

[10] Captain A. T. Mahan, *From Sail to Steam: Recollections of Naval Life* (New York: Harper and Brothers, 1907), 276; and Robert Seager II, *Alfred Thayer Mahan: The Man and His Letters* (Annapolis, Md.: Naval Institute Press, 1977), 205–8, 430 (hereinafter cited as *ATM*). See also Peter Karsten, *The Naval Aristocracy: The Golden Age of Annapolis and the Emergence of Modern American Navalism* (New York: Free Press, 1972), 277–317.
[11] Seager, *ATM*, 211
[12] Ibid., 206. See also Paul Kennedy, *The Rise and Fall of British Naval Mastery* (New York: Charles Scribner's Sons, 1976), 5–6.
[13] Mahan, *The Influence of Sea Power upon History*, 28. See also 82, 83–4.
[14] Ibid., 87.

of consistent policy perseveringly directed to one aim."[15] This point notwithstanding, he also believed that the experience of Britain was less relevant to his governmental argument because of the extent to which the actions of the British state were practically predetermined by the six principal conditions. Britain's insular geography had made it unnecessary for her leaders to maintain a large army for the purposes of national defense so long as she had sufficient naval strength to prevent a landing of foreign troops. Being small and surrounded by water also had meant that much of her population was bound to seek their living from maritime activity. The concentration of effort by Britain's rulers on overseas mercantile and colonial expansion supported by a powerful fleet had, in other words, been practically preordained by circumstance. "Singleness of purpose," Mahan observed, "was to some extent imposed."[16]

The position of France was different. A substantial army was required to defend the country's exposed land frontiers against invasion. On the other hand, she was no less and in some ways even more gifted than Britain with respect to those conditions favorable to the development of sea power. Thus the governments of France were confronted by a choice between the further development of an already considerable army for the purposes of national aggrandizement by land, and the minimization of army strength in order to channel resources toward overseas commercial, colonial, and naval growth. While Mahan admitted that France's continental position dictated the maintenance of a strong army, he was convinced that more could and should have been done for the navy. "France was constantly diverted," he argued "sometimes wisely and sometimes most foolishly, from the sea to projects of continental extension. These military efforts expended wealth; whereas a wiser and consistent use of her geographical position would have added to it."[17]

The French example also illustrated the importance of government action. Mahan described the initial buildup of the French navy under Louis XIV as "a most astonishing manifestation of the work which can be done by absolute government ably and systematically wielded."[18] "Yet all this wonderful growth," Mahan lamented, "forced by the action of the government, withered away like Jonah's gourd when the government's favor was withdrawn."[19] "The simplicity of form in an absolute monar-

---

[15] Ibid., 76.
[16] Ibid., 66.
[17] Ibid., 29
[18] Ibid., 70.
[19] Ibid., 72–3.

chy," he concluded, "thus brought out strongly how great the influence of government can be upon both the growth and decay of sea power."[20]

The consequences of poor state decision-making during the first half of the eighteenth century, Mahan contended, was "a false policy of continental extension" that "swallowed up the resources of the country, and was doubly injurious because, by leaving defenseless its colonies and commerce, . . . exposed the greatest source of wealth to be cut off."[21] On the other hand, the rebuilding of the fleet after the disastrous defeats in the Seven Years' War and aggressive deployment of this force enabled France to best Britain during the American Revolutionary War. "The profound humiliation of France," Mahan thus warned, "which reached its depths between 1760 and 1763, at which latter date she made peace, has an instructive lesson for the United States in this our period of commercial and naval decadence. We have been spared her humiliation; let us hope to profit by her subsequent example."[22]

In the closing pages of his first chapter, Mahan addressed his main practical concern. His great fear at this time was that the isolationist sentiments of the electorate would prevent the American state from building and maintaining the strong navy that he believed was essential to protect vital territorial and economic interests in a world in which competition between powerful nations was beginning to increase. "As the practical object of this inquiry," Mahan thus wrote, "is to draw from the lessons of history inferences applicable to one's own country and service, it is proper now to ask how far the conditions of the United States involve serious danger, and call for action on the part of the government, in order to build again her sea power."[23] His answer was clear: "the question is eminently one in which the influence of the government should make itself felt, to build up for the nation a navy which, if not capable of reaching distant countries, shall at least be able to keep clear the chief approaches to its own."[24]

Mahan provided a general account of the great Anglo-French conflicts of the late seventeenth and eighteenth centuries in the chapters that followed. Here, he presented political, political-economic, and

---

[20] Ibid., 74. For a perceptive if brief analysis of Mahan's views on French sea power and the role of government that was ignored by other scholars, see Bates McCluer Gilliam, "The World of Captain Mahan," (Ph.D. diss., Princeton University, 1961), 81–2.
[21] Mahan, *Influence of Sea Power upon History*, 75.
[22] Ibid., 76. Most of Mahan's sources, indeed, were French works, which is yet another indicator of where the emphasis of his inquiry lay.
[23] Ibid., 83–4.
[24] Ibid., 87.

governmental arguments largely in terms of French error or success. The critical event in chapters two and three was the decision by Louis XIV to reject the Leibnitz memorandum. This proposal of 1672 called for France to win control of the Mediterranean and the Eastern trade by action against Egypt, a policy of overseas expansion and commercial aggression based on naval power. The Leibnitz plan was turned down, however, in favor of a military offensive on the continent. "This decision, which killed Colbert and ruined the prosperity of France," Mahan argued, "was felt in its consequences from generation to generation afterward, as the great navy of England, in war after war, swept the seas, insured the growing wealth of the island kingdom through exhausting strifes, while drying up the external resources of French trade and inflicting consequent misery."[25]

Commenting on the outcome of the several wars of the 1670s, Mahan noted that "doubtless France could not forget her continental position, nor wholly keep free from continental wars; but it may be believed that if she had chosen the path of sea power, she might both have escaped many conflicts and borne those that were unavoidable with greater ease."[26] This was because "nations . . . decay when cut off from external activities and resources which at once draw out and support their internal powers."[27] Mahan acknowledged that the "overwhelming sea power of England was the determining factor" during the first half of the eighteenth century.[28] But he also saw this naval predominance as having come into being as much through French default as British design. "The position of France," he observed, "is in this peculiar, that of all the great powers she alone had a free choice; the others were more or less constrained to the land chiefly, or to the sea chiefly, for any movement outside their own borders; but she to her long continental frontier added a seaboard on three seas."[29]

The climax of Mahan's book was an examination of the naval duel between Britain and France during the American Revolution. This sub-

[25] Ibid., 107, 141–2.

[26] Ibid., 170.

[27] Ibid., 200. See also 197–8. For the particular damaging effects of loss of sea control upon state finance, see 227–8.

[28] Ibid., 209.

[29] Ibid., 226. Mahan later repudiated his argument with respect to French freedom of action, and indeed he had denied its existence in his recent correspondence, for which see Mahan to William H. Henderson, 30 November 1888, in *The Letters and Papers of Alfred Thayer Mahan*, ed. Robert Seager II and Doris Maguire, 3 vols. (Annapolis, Md.: Naval Institute Press, 1975), i: 671 (hereinafter cited as *LPATM*).

ject consumed no less than six of his fourteen chapters. Put another way, some 40 percent of the text was allocated to cover 4 percent of the chronology. Mahan argued that the absence of European continental entanglements, the rough equality of naval forces, and the extra-European objectives of the two hostile great powers meant that the confrontation could be characterized as "purely a maritime war."[30] In this conflict, a France undistracted by having to maintain substantial armies in Europe, and animated by an offensive naval strategy, used her battle fleet to compromise Britain's position in North America. The French commander Pierre-André de Suffren's brilliant actions in the Indian theater were given as another indicator of what the French navy could have done if led properly. And finally, on the opposite side, Mahan blamed France's failure to obtain "more substantial results" than it did on its unwillingness to press relentlessly for decisive action at sea, which could have destroyed British naval power when conditions were propitious.[31]

To summarize, the political-economic moral of *The Influence of Sea Power upon History* was that when circumstances favored both development by land or sea, which Mahan believed was the case of America in the late nineteenth century,[32] the leaders of states were well-advised to prefer the latter over the former on the grounds that the return on investment—that is to say success in war and increased national wealth as purchased by state spending—was higher. The governmental lesson was that in the case of France in the eighteenth and early nineteenth centuries, not following this course had enabled Britain to win important strategic victories that might otherwise have been defeats, while brief adherence had led to the creation of the United States. The world pre-eminence of Britain, the decadence of France, and the great development of American power were the highly visible ultimate manifestations of these outcomes in Mahan's own day, which served as testimonials to the apparent truth of his political argument.

THE INFLUENCE OF SEA POWER UPON THE FRENCH REVOLUTION AND EMPIRE, 1793–1812

Even prior to the publication of his first major book, Mahan had expressed his intention to produce a sequel that would cover the battle

---

[30] Mahan, *Influence of Sea Power upon History*, 505.
[31] Ibid., 538.
[32] Ibid., 38–9.

of Trafalgar.[33] But criticism of *The Influence of Sea Power upon History*, on the grounds that it had been based exclusively on secondary works, prompted him to make considerable use of printed correspondence and state papers in writing *The Influence of Sea Power upon the French Revolution and Empire*.[34] Exploitation of primary sources enabled Mahan to refine and deepen his analysis and to support it with more detailed narrative. The result was a substantially longer manuscript that had to be published in two volumes even though the amount of chronological ground to be covered was one-fifth that of its one-volume predecessor. The more significant difference between the progenitor and its sequel, however, was in the nature of its subject, which compelled Mahan to alter fundamentally the form and substance of his governmental argument.

The wars of the French Revolution and Empire again pitted France and Britain against one another, but not, as in previous wars, as actual or potential naval peers. By the outbreak of war, political upheaval had destroyed the officer corps, eroded the skills of the enlisted ranks, and disrupted the administration of the French navy, effects which proved to be irreversible. These factors, Mahan concluded, "were . . . surely the chief cause of the continuous and overwhelming overthrow" of that service in battle over the next two decades.[35] Having established the incapacity of France's fleet as a given, Mahan could not work the period in terms of faulty or correct French grand strategy, as he had previously, because the institutional weakness of the navy precluded success regardless of its deployment. As a consequence, he had no alternative but to replace the consideration of optimal policy choices for states with major maritime assets with an examination of whether a country supreme at sea was capable of defeating its opposite, a country supreme on land.[36]

Mahan expressed the essence of his political argument when he attributed Britain's immunity to invasion to the Royal Navy's close blockade of French naval bases. "The world," he wrote, "has never seen a more impressive demonstration of the influence of sea power upon its history. Those far distant, storm-beaten ships, upon which the Grand Army never looked, stood between it and the dominion of

---

[33] Seager, *ATM*, 199.
[34] Ibid., 213–4, 216.
[35] Captain A. T. Mahan, *The Influence of Sea Power upon the French Revolution and Empire, 1793–1812*, 2 vols. (Boston: Little, Brown, 1892), i: 68.
[36] The governmental argument of the previous book was echoed, however, for which see ibid., 203.

the world."[37] Mahan was no less eloquent in his political-economic argument:

> The strength of Great Britain could be said to lie in her commerce only as, and because, it was the external manifestation of the wisdom and strength of the British people, unhampered by any control beyond that of a government and institutions in essential sympathy with them. In the enjoyment of these blessings,—in their independence and untrammeled pursuit of wealth,—they were secured by their powerful navy; and so long as this breastplate was borne, unpierced, over the heart of the great organism, over the British islands themselves, Great Britain was—not invulnerable—but invincible. She could be hurt indeed, but she could not be slain.[38]

Mahan's governmental argument spoke not, as before, to the question of France choosing between expansion by land or by sea, but Britain's formulation and execution of a grand strategy of economic attrition.[39] "The true function of Great Britain in this long struggle," Mahan declared, "can scarcely be recognized unless there be a clear appreciation of the fact that a really great national movement, like the French Revolution, or a really great military power under an incomparable general, like the French empire under Napoleon, is not to be brought to terms by ordinary military successes, which simply destroy the organized force opposed."[40] To contain France, Mahan insisted, Britain "shut [Napoleon] off from the world, and by the same act prolonged her own powers of endurance beyond his power of aggression."[41] The genius of William Pitt the younger, the architect of this approach, Mahan thus concluded, was to equate the "security" of his own country with the "exhaustion" of the enemy.[42]

Mahan's political, political-economic, and governmental arguments were richly illustrated by his narrative. In his account of the wars of the

---

[37] Ibid., ii: 118.
[38] Ibid., i: 327.
[39] For Mahan's explicit separation of political-economic and governmental argument, see ibid., ii: 374–5. For Mahan's serious efforts to research the economic aspects of the war, see Mahan to Stephen B. Luce, 9 April 1890 and 27 October 1890, *LPATM*, ii: 2–3, 29.
[40] Ibid., ii: 409.
[41] Ibid., 411. See also 400–1.
[42] Ibid., 411.

French Revolution and Empire, the navies of Britain's main enemies, France and Spain, were first countered and neutralized, while secondary threats posed by the maritime forces of the Netherlands and Denmark were eliminated. The subsequent shattering of a combined Franco-Spanish battle fleet at Trafalgar largely removed even the possibility of serious challenge to British control of the oceans, thus securing the continued imposition of her blockade of the continent and the safety of her own overseas commerce. The latter was the economic foundation of the financial strength that sustained the armed forces of both Britain and its allies, while the former sapped the power of France and prompted it to take retaliatory economic action, which though damaging was not decisive and alienated European populations to France's serious political disadvantage.

Mahan had stressed the connection between naval and commercial activity in his previous book.[43] But in *The Influence of Sea Power upon the French Revolution and Empire*, these factors were related much more strongly by being synthesized into a single entity. Combined they constituted for Mahan a "wonderful and mysterious Power" that could be "seen to be a complex organism, endued [sic] with a life of its own, receiving and imparting countless impulses, moving in a thousand currents which twine in and around one another in infinite flexibility. . . . Attacked in every quarter and by every means, sought to be cut off alike from the sources and from the issues of its enterprise, it adapts itself with the readiness of instinct to every change. It yields here, it pushes there; it gives ground in one quarter, it advances in another; it bears heavy burdens, it receives heavy blows; but throughout all it lives and it grows."[44] Sea power, in other words, was in this volume transformed from a desirable policy option for certain countries into a self-sustaining system made up of both formal and informal elements. In these terms, it was not simply a political instrument but a new phenomenon that unconsciously but nonetheless effectively integrated the actions of the state with those of self-interested individuals and private corporations.

That the wars of the French Revolution and Empire could serve as a demonstration of the existence of sea power thus described was not inevitable, however. Mahan did not believe that Britain's victory over France was predetermined: "As in every contest where the opponents are closely matched, where power and discipline and leadership are

---

[43] Mahan, *Influence of Sea Power upon History*, esp. 225.
[44] Mahan, *French Revolution and Empire*, ii: 372–3.

nearly equal, there was a further question: which of the two would make the first and greatest mistakes, and how ready the other party was to profit by his errors. In so even a balance, the wisest prophet cannot foresee how the scale will turn."[45] The high degree of contingency that characterized the wars of the French Revolution and Empire meant that in spite of the fundamental importance of large structural factors, relatively small things could matter a great deal. That is to say, Mahan was convinced that the actions of individual humans counted, particularly those of gifted persons in positions of great responsibility.[46] Such may have been one of the main intellectual justifications for his decision to write a biography of Admiral Horatio Nelson, and to this task he turned as an alternative to his original intention of immediately writing a history of the War of 1812.[47]

THE LIFE OF NELSON: THE EMBODIMENT OF THE SEA POWER OF GREAT BRITAIN

Mahan's biography of Nelson covered much of the same chronology and subject as in the previous installment of the "Influence of Sea Power" series, and its political and political-economic arguments were thus identical.[48] What was different was the governmental argument, which was expressed in terms of Nelson as an agent of the state. To present this case, Mahan found it necessary to explicate his subject's "leading features of temperament, traits of thought, and motives of action" through a highly detailed narrative that he hoped would enable readers to understand the character of the man "by gradual familiarity even more than by formal effort."[49] This discursive approach, which again resulted in a two-volume presentation, was buttressed by a greater amount

---

[45] Ibid., 201.

[46] Napoleon and William Pitt (the younger) were the exemplars in politics; see ibid., 407, 411.

[47] Mahan, *From Sail to Steam*, 313, 317–23. For Mahan's later exclusion of his Nelson biography from the "Influence of Sea Power" series, a move motivated by opportunistic rather than intellectual reasoning, see Mahan to Little, Brown, 10 October 1906, *LPATM*, iii: 180–1.

[48] Captain A. T. Mahan, *Life of Nelson: The Embodiment of the Sea Power of Great Britain*, 2 vols. (Boston: Little, Brown, 1897), i: 97; ii: 62.

[49] Ibid., i: vii. For Mahan's alternative titles of this work, which reveal much about his underlying purposes, see Mahan to John M. Brown, 28 December 1896 and 26 January 1897, *LPATM*, ii: 480, 488.

of research in primary sources than had been required by his previous work.[50] Mahan was not an uncritical admirer of Nelson. He explored his character flaws vigorously[51] and qualified his virtues acutely.[52] But what really mattered to Mahan was Nelson's powers of command, especially within the particular context of naval warfare in the age of sail.

Detached service and slow communications meant that fleet commanders had to assume wide responsibilities for political action, logistics, and the commitment of forces to battle. For this reason, the formulation of sound strategy by leaders of state and the naval high command was only the beginning of effective national policy; a very great deal depended upon the execution of a broad commission. To carry out his brief, an admiral in the ordinary course of things had to possess a combination of political, administrative, and military skills rare in any single man, while a great naval leader in addition required these talents to be developed to a pronounced degree. Nelson, Mahan maintained, exhibited mastery in all three areas. The historian awarded his subject high marks for his political judgment when confronted by awkward circumstances and his ability to manage the supply of a fleet in the face of great difficulties.[53] His most fulsome praise, however, was reserved for Nelson's consistent willingness to choose a course of action that would result in decisive engagement with, and destruction of, the enemy.

Mahan's emphasis on this particular quality stemmed from his belief that there existed a "too common, almost universal, weakness" among naval officers that deterred "men from a bold initiative, from assuming responsibility, from embracing opportunity."[54] As a consequence, French fleets on many occasions escaped serious harm, forcing Britain "to bear the uncertainties, exposure, and expense of a difficult and protracted defensive."[55] Aversiveness to risk on the part of most men was to be explained by the complex and uncertain conditions under which naval decision-making had to be undertaken, but to Mahan these were factors to be overcome, not excuses for indecisiveness.[56] "It is not certainties, but chances, that determine the propriety of military

---

[50] Seager, *ATM*, 437.
[51] Mahan, *Nelson*, i: 313–4.
[52] Ibid., i: 32–3, 138, 151, 208, 210, 234, 258, 295–6, 440; ii: 129, 139, 141, 163.
[53] Ibid., i: 190, 297; ii: 197, 207–9.
[54] Ibid., i: 452–3.
[55] Ibid., i: 103.
[56] Ibid., ii: 164.

action,"[57] he wrote, also stating first that the "risks springing from misplaced caution [could be] more ruinous than the most daring venture."[58]

Mahan did not attribute Nelson's success to unalloyed aggressiveness, however. "Circumspection," he remarked, "was in him as marked a trait as ardor."[59] The admiral's judgments on one occasion, Mahan observed, "if rapid, [were] not precipitate."[60] On another, he noted that Nelson showed "an instructive combination of rapidity and caution, of quick comprehension of the situation, with an absence of all precipitation; no haste incompatible with perfect carefulness, no time lost, either by hesitation or by preparations postponed."[61] In Nelson, a "sagacious appreciation of conditions [was] combined with so much exalted resolution and sound discretion."[62] "Yet do not imagine," Nelson writes in a letter quoted by Mahan, that "I am one of those hot brained people, who fight at an immense disadvantage, without an adequate object."[63]

In addition to the ability to assess the odds with high intelligence tempered by long experience, Nelson, in Mahan's view, believed in the vital importance of seeking a decision through battle as a matter of principle. When confronted by the confusion of war, Mahan asserted, "the only sure guide to a man's feet is principle; and Nelson's principle was the destruction of the French fleet. No other interest, his own least of all, could divert him from it. For it he was willing not only to sacrifice fortune, but to risk renown; and so, amid troubles manifold, he walked steadfastly in the light of the single eye."[64] It was "strength of conviction," Mahan maintained, that lifted Nelson "from the plane of doubt, where unaided reason alone would leave him, to that of unhesitating action, incapable of looking backward." "It is such conviction," he continued, "in which opinion rather possesses a man than is possessed by him, that exalts genius above talent, and imbues faith with a power which reason has not in her gift."[65]

Nelson's guiding principle was justified by Britain's strategic predicament. His country's survival depended upon the conversion of naval su-

[57] Ibid., i: 358.
[58] Ibid., i: 326.
[59] Ibid., ii: 294.
[60] Ibid., ii: 302.
[61] Ibid., i: 347. For the characterization of Suffren in similar terms, see Mahan, *Influence of Sea Power upon History*, 426.
[62] Mahan, *Nelson*, ii: 306.
[63] Ibid., ii: 305.
[64] Ibid., ii: 271.
[65] Ibid., ii: 303.

periority, which had been produced by larger circumstances, into naval supremacy, which could be achieved only through the exploitation of a few, elusive opportunities for battle. In the absence of supremacy, mere superiority conferred no more than immediate security held hostage to an unpropitious future. The elimination of the enemy fleet, on the other hand, not only vitiated a dangerous military threat but was likely to bring political benefits of manifold and considerable significance, which could prove decisive in a war in which the balance between the contending powers was so even. Nelson's convictions with respect to offensive use of a British fleet can thus be seen to have been founded upon profound political and strategic understanding.

But right thinking and faith were still insufficient explanation for Mahan of Nelson's genius: "Reasoning of a very high order illuminates Nelson's mental processes, but it is not in the power of reason, when face to face with emergency, to bridge the chasm that separates perception, however clear, from the inward conviction which alone sustains the loftiest action."[66] To connect the two during a time of crisis demanded moral courage, which Nelson, Mahan was convinced, possessed in abundance.[67] Mahan's governmental argument, in short, was that intelligence, understanding of sound principles, and resolution—the qualities that had made Nelson the "Embodiment of the Sea Power of Great Britain"—were the cardinal virtues of effective naval leadership. The relationship of these qualities to the larger forces of history was explained by Mahan in a March 1899 letter to James Ford Rhodes, a distinguished fellow historian: men "both control events and are controlled by them. . . . Between events and man's will there is a resultant of forces."[68]

SEA POWER IN ITS RELATIONS TO THE WAR OF 1812

The enormous labor of researching and writing the Nelson biography caused Mahan "extreme difficulty."[69] Fatigue, indeed, may explain the suggestion, if it was that, expressed in the opening pages of the Nelson volumes, that they were the final installment of the author's "Influence

---

[66] Ibid., ii: 324.
[67] Ibid., i: 189.
[68] Seager, *ATM*, 438.
[69] Mahan correspondence, quoted in Seager, *ATM*, 437.

of Sea Power" series.[70] But retirement in 1896 relieved him of the burdens of a naval career, and in 1897, only a few months after the publication of the Nelson biography, Mahan began work on *Sea Power in Its Relations to the War of 1812*. As had happened before, Mahan improved his research over that of his preceding book, enabling him to broaden and deepen the analysis and present a detailed narrative. The predictable result was another lengthy study that was first serialized in *Scribner's Magazine* in eleven parts over the course of 1903 and 1904 and then was published in two volumes in 1905.[71]

Mahan's political argument was presented inversely—that is, not as a study of the benefits of naval strength, but as an examination of the disastrous consequences to the United States of naval unpreparedness. Mahan thus observed in his preface that whereas in his previous books he had examined sea power as "a positive and commanding element in the history of the world," in his latest effort he would handle the subject in terms of its absence having had "the influence of a negative quantity upon national history."[72] By framing his treatment this way, Mahan addressed the question of American naval weakness directly through its own history instead of indirectly by means of analogy to foreign example. The opportunity to write critically about the U.S. Navy may have been one of the main reasons—apart from financial gain—that he took on the task in the first place.

Mahan's political-economic argument, like his political one, was presented from a perspective that was the opposite of the one he had assumed previously. American commercial prosperity, he maintained, depended upon the security of maritime communications. When these were disrupted by the British blockade, the general economy suffered severely, to the detriment of state revenues upon which the sustenance of American armed forces was based. "Money, credit, is the life of war; lessen it, and vigor flags; destroy it, and resistance dies."[73] Mahan's governmental argument was that both the outbreak of an unnecessary war and its disastrous consequences were attributable to naval unprepared-

[70] Mahan, *Nelson*, i: v.
[71] Seager, *ATM*, 564–9. See also Mahan to John M. Brown, 10 February 1897, *LPATM*, ii: 491.
[72] Captain A. T. Mahan, *Sea Power in Its Relations to the War of 1812*, 2 vols. (Boston: Little, Brown, 1905), i: v.
[73] Ibid., i: 285. Later repeated word for word in A. T. Mahan, "The Hague Conference of 1907, and the Question of Immunity for Belligerent Merchant Shipping," *National Review* (July 1907), reprinted in Mahan, *Some Neglected Aspects of War*, 190. See also Mahan to Theodore Roosevelt, 27 December 1904, *LPATM*, iii: 113; and Mahan to Elihu Root, 20 April 1906, *LPATM*, iii: 158.

ness. His lengthy treatment of the economic, diplomatic, and legal an-
tecedents of the outbreak of hostilities illustrated the weakness of the
negotiating position of a state that lacked substantial naval force. "Having failed to create before the war, a competent navy," he wrote, "capable of seizing opportunity, when offered, to act against hostile divisions
throughout the world, it was not possible afterwards to retrieve this
mistake."[74]

Naval competency, Mahan was careful to explain, did not demand
the building of a large fleet. "The lesson to be deduced," he stated,

> is not that the country at that time should have sought to main-
> tain a navy approaching equality to the British. [Given] the state
> of national population and revenue, it was no more possible to
> attempt this than it would be expedient to do it now, under the
> present immense development of resources and available wealth.
> What had been possible during the decade preceding the war,—
> had the nation so willed,—was to place the navy on such a foot-
> ing, in numbers and constitution, as would have made persistence
> in the course Great Britain was following impolitic to the verge
> of madness, because it would add to her war embarrassments the
> activity of an imposing maritime enemy, at the threshold of her
> most valuable markets,—the West Indies,—three thousand miles
> away from her own shores and from the seat of her principal and
> necessary warfare.[75]

A modest navy could be strong enough to deter the leading naval power
when geographical and other circumstances were taken into account—
this was Mahan's conception of a naval strategy appropriate to the
United States at the conclusion of his systematic study of naval warfare
in the seventeenth, eighteenth, and early nineteenth centuries.[76]

---

[74] Mahan, *1812*, i: 310–1.
[75] Ibid., ii: 208–9; see also 212.
[76] Ibid., i: v. Mahan did call for a navy equal to that of Britain in the event of the construction of a canal through the Central American isthmus in casual letters written a
decade before, for which see Mahan to Samuel A. Ashe, 12 March 1880 and 11 March
1885, *LPATM*, i: 482.

CHAPTER THREE

Strategic and Professional Argument in
the "Influence of Sea Power" Series

But when you have been at sea as long as I have . . . you will know there
is a great deal more than mere seamanship required of a captain. Any
damned tarpaulin can manage a ship in a storm . . . and any housewife in
breeches can keep the decks clean and the falls just so; but it needs a
headpiece . . . and true bottom and steadiness, as well as conduct, to be
the captain of a man-o'-war: and these are qualities not to be found in
every Johnny-come-lately.

—Patrick O'Brian, *Master and Commander*

The colonel says, "Just five minutes," and then he goes to the window
and he stops and thinks. That's what [officers are] very good at—making
decisions. I thought it was very remarkable how a problem of whether or
not information as to how the [atomic] bomb works should be in the
Oak Ridge plant had to be decided and *could* be decided in five minutes.
So I have a great deal of respect for these military guys, because I never
can decide anything very important in any length of time at all.

—Richard P. Feynman, *"Surely You're Joking, Mr. Feynman!":*
Adventures of a Curious Character

PRINCIPLES OF STRATEGY

In the introduction to *The Influence of Sea Power upon History*, Mahan
maintained that the study of the historical record could serve as a
means of acquiring practical insight into the nature of naval strategy
because, unlike tactics, strategy was much less affected by technological

change.[1] He was nevertheless wary of the dangers of applying the past to the present through simple reasoning by analogy. "In tracing resemblances," Mahan wrote, "there is a tendency not only to overlook points of difference, but to exaggerate points of likeness,—to be fanciful."[2] Thus he argued that the proper function of sound strategic history was to provide not just precedents—that is, examples—but also principles, or what could be called fundamental truths about operational dynamics. A "precedent is different from and less valuable than a principle," Mahan observed. "The former may be originally faulty, or may cease to apply through change of circumstances; the latter has its root in the essential nature of things, and, however various its application as conditions change, remains a standard to which action must conform to attain success."[3]

For Mahan, naval strategy in war was concerned with the functions of navies, their objectives and deployments, logistics, communications, and in particular the form and priority of commerce-raiding.[4] From *The Influence of Sea Power upon History* onward, Mahan's strategic argument was consistently based upon the principle of concentration of force and consideration of logistical context, which Mahan had borrowed from the military writing of Jomini.[5] Mahan applied the concept of concentration of force widely and in various guises. In addition to its pure forms—"numbers annihilate" or "never divide the fleet"—there were first- and second-order derivative propositions relating to the desirability of taking the offensive, decisive battle, and the relative ineffectiveness of commerce-raiding by cruisers as a substitute for control of the sea by battleships. Because of the continuity of Mahan's strategic argument, the following analysis examines its various categories rather than in a volume-by-volume presentation.

The fundamental flaw of British strategy in the American Revolution, Mahan argued, was a failure to concentrate naval forces and use them to pursue a vigorous offensive.[6] He criticized Nelson for formulating a plan in 1801 that lacked "the necessary corrective to an ill-

---

[1] Alfred Thayer Mahan, *The Influence of Sea Power upon History, 1660–1783* (Boston: Little, Brown, 1890), 7–10. See also 88.
[2] Ibid., 5.
[3] Ibid., 7.
[4] Ibid., 8.
[5] Jomini's concept of the strategic value of central position and interior lines was also utilized by Mahan, but not frequently, and will not be considered in this analysis. For its mention in the "Influence of Sea Power" series, see Mahan, *Influence of Sea Power upon History*, 30. For his dismissal of it as a proposition of secondary value, see Captain A. T. Mahan, *Naval Strategy: Compared and Contrasted with the Principles and Practice of Military Operations on Land* (Boston: Little, Brown, 1911), 53.
[6] Mahan, *Influence of Sea Power upon History*, 394, 396, 414.

conceived readiness to sub-divide."[7] Mahan attributed British success in
the Trafalgar campaign of 1805 in large part to their steadfast concentration of force in European waters in spite of French feints in distant
seas.[8] In his history of the War of 1812, he insisted that wars were won
not by "rambling operations, or naval duels," or "by brilliant individual
feats of gallantry or skill, by ships or men," but by "the massing of superior forces," or "by force massed and handled in skillful combination."[9]
Mahan took some pains to qualify his advocacy of principle: "All military
experience concurs in the general rule of co-operative action; and this
means concentration, under the liberal definition before given—unity of
purpose and subordination to a central control. General rules, however,
must be intelligently applied to particular circumstances. . . ."[10]

Mahan held up conclusive engagement with the main force of the
enemy as an ideal to counteract what he perceived as a tendency toward
excessive caution in most men. In addition, he was convinced that the
destruction of the enemy's means of fighting, as opposed to the mere
frustration of his immediate actions, conferred strategic benefits that
more than repaid the greater difficulty of the task.[11] Mahan thus praised
aggressiveness[12] and reproved defensive attitudes that promoted inactivity.[13] He recognized, on the other hand, that decisive battles would
be difficult if not impossible to bring about; even when the opportunity
was presented, the risks might not justify their taking, and there were
exceptions to the rule.[14] For example, Mahan argued on one occasion
that the capture of the enemy's port and not the defeat of its fleet was
the preferred course of action.[15] Mahan believed above all that battle
always had to have a worthwhile strategic objective, and he even expressed a preference for a defeat that had favorable larger consequences
to "the sterile glory of fighting battles merely to win them."[16]

[7] Captain A. T. Mahan, *The Life of Nelson: The Embodiment of the Sea Power of Great Britain*, 2 vols. (Boston: Little, Brown, 1897), ii: 129.
[8] Captain A. T. Mahan, *The Influence of Sea Power upon the French Revolution and Empire, 1793–1812*, 2 vols. (Boston: Little, Brown, 1892), ii: 157–8.
[9] Captain A. T. Mahan, *Sea Power in Its Relations to the War of 1812*, 2 vols. (Boston: Little, Brown, 1905), i: v; ii: 101.
[10] Ibid., i: 319. See also 315–6.
[11] Mahan, *Influence of Sea Power upon History*, 338–9, 425, 478, 534, 538; Mahan, *French Revolution and Empire*, i: 229; and Mahan, *Nelson*, i: 103, 171; ii: 196.
[12] Mahan, *1812*, i: 298.
[13] Mahan, *French Revolution and Empire*, i: 199, 201.
[14] Ibid., i: 229; Mahan, *Nelson*, i: 171, 225, 264, 452–3.
[15] Mahan, *1812*, ii: 59.
[16] Mahan, *Nelson*, ii: 323. For the attribution of the phrase to Jomini, see Captain A. T. Mahan, *From Sail to Steam: Recollections of Naval Life* (New York: Harper and Brothers, 1907) 283.

Mahan disliked amphibious operations on the grounds that they did not produce significant benefits and were dangerous to the forces involved and thus should be avoided as a waste of resources. He dismissed Nelson's predilection for such schemes as "a fad" at best.[17] At worst, Mahan believed that they constituted an "erroneous military conception which colored much of [Nelson's] thought," involving "ex-centric movements in an enemy's rear, by bodies comparatively small, out of supporting distance from the rest of the army, and resting upon no impregnable base."[18] Besides violating the fundamental principle of concentration of force, and posing logistical burdens that diverted effort away from dealing with an opponent's main fleet, they risked skilled manpower. Common sense, Mahan believed, militated against "the pernicious practice of jeopardizing the personnel of a fleet, the peculiar trained force so vitally necessary, and so hard to replace, in petty operations on shore."[19] A similar concern with the misappropriation of valuable labor for tasks of tertiary importance prompted Mahan to note—with respect to the inadvisability of increasing the numbers of small craft for coastal operations—that "the flotilla could not be manned without diminishing the cruisers in commission, which were far short of the ideal number."[20]

Mahan's views on commerce-raiding as a strategy require the most careful statement and consideration of context. His fundamental position was that the very existence of navies was justified primarily by their ability to defend their own commerce and to attack that of their opponent. Insofar as the latter was concerned, Mahan was opposed not to commerce-raiding *per se*, but rather to the "general inadequacy of such a warfare when not supported by fleets."[21] At the very least, Mahan argued, commerce-destroying warfare, "to be destructive, must be seconded by a squadron warfare, and by divisions of ships-of-the-line; which, forcing the enemy to unite his forces, permit the cruisers to make fortunate attempts upon his trade."[22] "To assume a menacing attitude at many points," he wrote elsewhere, "to give effect to the men-

---

[17] Mahan, *French Revolution and Empire*, i: 208.
[18] Mahan, *Nelson*, i: 208. See also 213 and 227.
[19] Ibid., 451.
[20] Ibid., ii: 132.
[21] Mahan, *Influence of Sea Power upon History*, 179.
[22] Ibid., 196. See also Mahan, *French Revolution and Empire*, i: 179–80. For the central role of attacks on commerce in Mahan's thinking about his own day, see Mahan to the editor of the *New York Times*, 15 November 1898, in *The Letters and Papers of Alfred Thayer Mahan*, 3 vols., ed. Robert Seager II and Doris Maguire (Annapolis, Md.: Naval Institute Press, 1975), ii: 612 (hereinafter cited as *LPATM*).

ace by frequent and vigorous sorties, to provoke thus a dispersion of the enemy's superior force, that he may be led to expose detachments to attack by greater numbers,—such must be the outline of conduct laid down for the weaker navy."[23]

The complete interdiction of enemy trade, which was essential if sea power was to exert its full effects on the outcome of a war, could be achieved only by a commercial blockade whose inviolacy had to be guaranteed by heavy units skillfully deployed. Mahan favored blockade of the enemy's coasts over attacks on the high seas because he believed that it was "the beginnings and endings of commercial routes, rather than the intermediate stretch, which most favor enterprises against an enemy's trade."[24] He argued further that it was not "the taking of individual ships or convoys, be they few or many, that strikes down the money power of a nation; it is the possession of that overbearing power on the sea which drives the enemy's flag from it, or allows it to appear only as a fugitive; and which by controlling the great common, closes the highways by which commerce moves to and from the enemy's shores."[25] This was especially true if one's opponent possessed both "a widespread healthy commerce and a powerful navy," in which case Mahan declared that "only by military command of the sea by prolonged control of the strategic centres of commerce" could an attack on trade be decisive, and that "such control can be wrung from a powerful navy only by fighting and overcoming it."[26]

Mahan's early propensity to dismiss commerce-raiding by cruisers as an activity incapable of achieving decisive results was later reinforced by his conclusion that convoy was a highly effective means of protecting merchant shipping. "A convoy is doubtless a much larger object than a single ship," he observed in the first volume of his study of the War of 1812, "but vessels thus concentrated in place and in time are more apt to pass wholly unseen than the same number sailing independently, and so scattered over wide expanses of sea."[27] In the second volume of the same work, Mahan wrote,

> The limited success of the frigates in their attempts against
> British trade has been noted, and attributed to the general fact

---

[23] Mahan, *French Revolution and Empire*, i: 180.
[24] Mahan, *1812*, ii: 229.
[25] Mahan, *Influence of Sea Power upon History*, 138. See also Mahan, *1812*, ii: 126.
[26] Mahan, *Influence of Sea Power upon History*, 539–40. See also 229–30.
[27] Mahan, *1812*, i: 409.

that their cruises were confined to the more open sea, upon the highways of commerce. These were now traveled by British ships under strict laws of convoy, the effect of which was not merely to protect the several flocks concentrated under their particular watchdogs, but to strip the sea of those isolated vessels, that in time of peace rise in irregular but frequent succession above the horizon, covering the face of the deep with a network of tracks. These solitary wayfarers were now to be found only as rare exceptions to the general rule, until the port of destination was approached.[28]

Mahan's dismissal of commerce-raiding by cruisers as the primary form of naval warfare was also a response to certain of its characteristics peculiar to his country and his day. Nineteenth-century American proponents of commerce-raiding expected it to be carried out by individual cruisers or converted merchant vessels—that is, by a force that did not require extensive peacetime exercise in combined maneuver and that supposedly could be improvised out of ill-trained crews and long-idle men-of-war or formerly private commercial ships after the outbreak of hostilities.[29] When Mahan denounced attacks on trade that were unsupported by a battle fleet, therefore, he was opposing not merely the efficacy of the activity, but the notion that the nautical equivalent of a land militia could serve effectively in the place of a standing navy.[30] The main issue here, in other words, was a choice between what Mahan described as "a most dangerous delusion" that was being "presented in the fascinating garb of cheapness"[31] and what he frequently referred to as "organized force."[32]

---

[28] Ibid., ii: 216. See also 130.

[29] Ibid., i: 286. For the importance of fleet drill, see Mahan, *Influence of Sea Power upon History*, 465.

[30] Mahan, *1812*, i: 286.

[31] Mahan, *Influence of Sea Power upon History*, 539. See also 132.

[32] Ibid., 112, 325, 326, 373, 416, 465, 538; Mahan, *1812*, ii: 118, 120, 132. For the attribution of the phrase to Jomini, see Captain A. T. Mahan, *From Sail to Steam*, 283. For Mahan's use of the term in his other works, see A.T. Mahan, "The Relations of the United States to Their New Dependencies," *Engineering Magazine* (January 1899), reprinted in Alfred T. Mahan, *Lessons of the War with Spain and Other Articles* (Boston: Little, Brown, 1899), 251; A. T. Mahan, "The Effect of Asiatic Conditions upon World Policies," *North American Review* (November 1900), reprinted in A. T. Mahan, *The Problem of Asia and Its Effect upon International Policies* (New York: Little, Brown, 1900), 191; A. T. Mahan, "Considerations Governing the Disposition of Navies," *National Review* (July 1902), reprinted in A. T. Mahan, *Retrospect and Prospect: Studies in International Relations Naval and Political* (London: Sampson Low, Marston, 1902), 168; and A. T. Mahan, *Naval Strategy* (Boston: Little, Brown, 1911), 176, 254, 260.

Mahan's preference for disciplined and concentrated forces over ill-trained and scattered local militias also underlay his aversion to coastal defense through gunboats. The manning of armed small craft, he observed, was characterized in general by a "comparatively easy standard of discipline and training,"[33] which in the case of the gunboat fleet of the United States at the time of the War of 1812 produced conditions that were "deleterious to the professional character of officers and seamen."[34] Large numbers of small vessels, Mahan also argued, were "capable of minute subdivision and wide dispersal" that dissipated force in the vain hope that such comprehensive but weak deployment would provide adequate protection for most if not all of a country's coastal maritime assets.[35] This did not mean, however, that Mahan rejected coastal defense in principle, but only its practice in a certain form for the unattainable goal of nearly perfect if not absolute security.

Effective coastal defense, Mahan insisted, was to be found not in dispersed flotilla craft, but in a combination of strong local land defenses and a fleet of warships that was capable either of drawing enemy forces away from shores through offensive action on the high seas or of forcing them to be concentrated against a powerful—if inferior—fleet in being and thus hindering eccentric operations against coastal shipping. "Seaports," Mahan maintained, "should defend themselves; the sphere of the fleet is on the open sea, its object offense rather than defense, its objective the enemy's shipping wherever it can be found."[36] "Navies do not dispense with fortifications nor with armies," he argued elsewhere, "but when wisely handled, they may save their country the strain which comes when these have to be called into play,—when war, once remote, now thunders at the gates, and the sea, the mother of prosperity, is shut off."[37] Finally, Mahan noted that while a small fleet could not "drive away a body numerically much stronger," it could nonetheless "compel the enemy to keep united" and thus minimize "the injury caused to a coast-line by the dispersion of the enemy's force."[38]

In the first three installments of the "Influence of Sea Power" series, Mahan maintained that logistical efficiency was essential to naval suc-

---

[33] Mahan, *Nelson*, i: 224.
[34] Mahan, *1812*, ii: 154–5.
[35] Mahan, *Nelson*, ii: 131.
[36] Mahan, *Influence of Sea Power upon History*, 453.
[37] Mahan, *French Revolution and Empire*, i: 341–2.
[38] Mahan, *1812*, i: 299.

cess, that the achievement of efficiency was difficult, and that its accomplishment was deserving of the highest praise, but that logistical problems could also serve as a pretext for inactivity that could compromise operations. He thus insisted, for example, that "depots of supplies" that were "always near at hand" were "essential to a fleet,"[39] emphasized the importance of Nelson's gifts as a logistician,[40] accepted the fact that logistical considerations could force the pursuit of a cautious policy that might otherwise have been open to condemnation,[41] and recognized that logistics could determine where and for how long fleets could operate.[42] Yet Mahan also observed of the behavior of the French admiral Suffren during the American Revolution that "no military lesson is more instructive nor of more enduring value than the rapidity and ingenuity with which he, without a port or supplies, continually refitted his fleet and took the field, while his slower enemy was dawdling over his repairs."[43]

In the *Influence of Sea Power upon History*, Mahan noted that the operational effectiveness of the French and Spanish navies during the American Revolution was influenced heavily by "inefficient administration and preparation."[44] He declined to discuss these matters at length, however, on the grounds that such explanation would obscure his presentation of strategic argument: "Questions of preparation and administration, . . . though of deep military interest and importance, are very different from the strategic plan or method adopted by the allied courts in selecting and attacking their objectives, and so compassing the objects of the war; and their examination would not only extend this discussion unreasonably, but would also obscure the strategic question by heaping up unnecessary details foreign to its subject."[45] In his subsequent study of the French Revolution and Empire, the fundamental importance of defective French administration was conceded at the outset and then set aside.[46]

---

[39] Mahan, *French Revolution and Empire*, i: 184. See also 371; and Mahan, *Influence of Sea Power upon History*, 451, 514.
[40] Mahan, *Nelson*, ii: 197–200, 207–9, 215, 244, 314.
[41] Ibid., i: 250.
[42] Ibid., i: 320; ii: 329. See also Mahan, *French Revolution and Empire*, ii: 107–8.
[43] Mahan, *Influence of Sea Power upon History*, 443. For other passages on logistical difficulty as an excuse for inactivity, see 477–8.
[44] Ibid., 536.
[45] Ibid., 537.
[46] Mahan, *French Revolution and Empire*, i: 38–68.

UNCERTAINTIES PECULIAR TO THE SEA

Mahan's nuanced and qualified presentation of his strategic argument was punctuated by admonitions that operational planning had to take account of natural forces such as the weather.[47] In the Indian Ocean, Mahan observed, "the trade-winds, or monsoons, . . . had strategic bearing."[48] Along the Atlantic seaboard of the northeastern United States, Mahan noted, "the long nights and stormy seas of winter . . . afforded to coasters a more secure protection than friendly guns."[49] Storms could change unpredictably the outcome of battles and campaigns. Mahan pointed out that during the American Revolution, a major battle between the French and the British in August 1781 was prevented when "a violent gale of wind dispersed the fleets."[50] Describing the destruction of French ships by tempests during the French Revolution, he wrote that "the stars, or rather the winds, in their courses had fought for Great Britain; but in no wise did [Great Britain] owe anything to her own efforts."[51]

Another major problem was the difficulty of knowing the whereabouts of the enemy once he had left his bases. "Armies pass through countries more or less inhabited by a stationary population," he explained, "and they leave behind them traces of their march. Fleets move through a desert over which wanderers flit, but where they do not remain; and as the waters close behind them, an occasional waif from the decks may indicate their passage, but tells nothing of their course. The sail spoken by the pursuer may know nothing of the pursued, which yet passed the point of parley but a few days or hours before."[52] Given the unlikelihood of successful interception of an enemy on the high seas, Mahan argued that if the enemy evaded a watch on his ports, the next best thing was "to get first to the enemy's destination and await him there; but this implies a knowledge of his intentions which may not always be obtainable."[53] And, indeed, unreliable intelligence misled

---

[47] For particularly revealing examples of Mahan's meticulous research with respect to meteorological and oceanographic detail, see Mahan to Richardson Clover, 15 and 21 March 1892, *LPATM*, ii: 66–7; and Mahan to Joseph E. Craig, 11 February 1898, *LPATM*, ii: 540–1.
[48] Mahan, *Influence of Sea Power upon History*, 518. See also 458; and Mahan, *French Revolution and Empire*, i: 343–4.
[49] Mahan, *1812*, ii: 192. See also Mahan, *Influence of Sea Power upon History*, 300–2, 527.
[50] Mahan, *Influence of Sea Power upon History*, 362. See also Mahan, *Nelson*, ii: 24, 278.
[51] Mahan, *French Revolution and Empire*, i: 164. See also 219, 256; and Mahan, *Nelson*, ii: 269.
[52] Mahan, *Influence of Sea Power upon History*, 520
[53] Ibid., 521.

Nelson at a critical moment during his pursuit of the French fleet during the Trafalgar campaign, which allowed his quarry to escape, if only temporarily.[54]

The vagaries of the natural elements and the vastness of the ocean spaces together—in the absence during the age of sail of adequate technical means of overcoming their effects—created what Mahan called "uncertainties peculiar to the sea."[55] These same factors were probably in his mind when he later observed that "the conditions of sea war then introduced so many varying quantities" that it was impossible to state the chances of success of a particular operation.[56] Unpredictable occurrences could favor or disfavor action to such a degree, Mahan warned, that even "the best-laid plans . . . may fail."[57] He quoted Nelson's lament that he could not "command winds and weather" and that a sea officer—unlike a commander on land—could not "form plans" but only hope "to embrace the happy moment which now and then offers . . . this day, not for a month, and perhaps never."[58] Mahan also cited Nelson's warning that "nothing is sure in a Sea Fight beyond all others."[59]

PROFESSIONAL IMPLICATIONS OF UNCERTAINTY

The proneness of naval operations to misadventure did not mean that careful planning was unnecessary, however. Mahan still called for "sagacious appreciation of well-known facts" and preparation "proportioned to the difficulties to be encountered" as obligatory procedures; "heedlessness of conditions, or recklessness of dangers," he wrote, "defeat effort everywhere."[60] In the entire "Influence of Sea Power" series, there is arguably no harsher rebuke of leadership failure than that applied to Captain James Lawrence, a naval martyr of the War of 1812:

> The American captain took the most promising method open to him for achieving success, and carried into the fight a ship's company which was not so untrained but that, had some luck favored him, instead of going the other way, there was a fighting chance

[54] Mahan, *Nelson*, ii: 299.
[55] Mahan, *French Revolution and Empire*, i: v.
[56] Ibid., ii: 182.
[57] Mahan, *Influence of Sea Power upon History*, 471.
[58] Mahan, *Nelson*, i: 225.
[59] Ibid., ii: 344.
[60] Mahan, *1812*, i: 354.

of victory. More cannot be claimed for him. He had no right, under the conditions, voluntarily to seek the odds against him, established by [British captain Philip] Broke's seven years of faithful and skilful command. Except in material force, the "Chesapeake" was a ship much inferior to the "Shannon," as a regiment newly enlisted is to one that has seen service; and the moment things went seriously wrong she could not retrieve herself. This her captain must have known; and to the accusation of his country and his service that he brought upon them a mortification which endures to this day, the only reply is that he died "sword in hand." This covers the error of the dead, but cannot justify the example to the living.[61]

But on the other hand, given the large play of contingency and the vital importance at certain times that something be done in the face of grave risks, inflexible decision-making could be dangerous, if not disastrous. "Jomini," Mahan thus observed, "doubtless may be considered somewhat too absolute and pedantic in his insistence upon definite formulation of principles."[62] Bridging the chasm between the limitations of even the most sophisticated theory and the varying and unpredictable demands of practice required the exercise of good judgment. Mahan's naval professional argument was that the leadership of navies should be entrusted to men who possessed it, historically based education promoted its development, and close association with technical or administrative activity disfavored its development. At the core of this set of convictions was the notion that the proper study of naval history would counteract the propensity of officers to act only when certain about what to do—a state of mind unlikely to be achieved during a campaign or battle.

The need for certainty as the basis for decision-making in war, Mahan maintained, was "the great snare of the mere engineer."[63] A grasp of sound principles, on the other hand, could provide "the vivid inspiration that enables its happy possessor, at critical moments, to see and follow the bright clear line, which, like a ray of light at midnight, shining among manifold doubtful indications, guides his steps."[64] "But for success in war," Mahan also insisted, "the indispensable complement of intellectual grasp and insight is a moral power, which enables a man to

---

[61] Ibid., ii: 145.
[62] Mahan, *Nelson*, i: 235.
[63] Ibid., 125.
[64] Ibid., 125.

trust the inner light,—to have faith,—a power which dominates hesitation, and sustains action, in the most tremendous emergencies."[65] By moral power, he meant above all the courage to assume responsibility for actions whose outcomes were both uncertain and potentially dire.

The "men are rare," Mahan wrote, "who in an unforeseen emergency can see, and at once take the right course, especially if, being subordinates, they incur responsibility."[66] He admired the British admiral Sir John Jervis (Lord St. Vincent) not only for his "cool, sound, and rapid professional judgment" and "steady, unflinching determination to succeed," but also for "a perfect fearlessness of responsibility such as Nelson also showed."[67] As for the latter, Mahan attributed his "accuracy of mental perception," "power of penetrating to the root of a matter," and capacity of "disregarding the unessential details and fastening solely on decisive features" to Nelson's recognition that productive action was essential to the survival of his country, or in other words, to his "sobering sense of responsibility."[68] In addition, naval leaders needed to possess a capacity to assume responsibility for diplomatic initiatives as well as deployments in battle. "Political courage in an officer abroad," Mahan wrote, quoting Nelson, "is as highly necessary as military courage."[69]

Mahan's emphasis on the importance of the ability to exercise independent judgment, however, was balanced by certain large reservations:

> It is possible to recognize the sound policy, the moral courage, and the correctness of . . . a step in the particular instance without at all sanctioning the idea that an officer may be justified in violating orders, because he thinks it right. The justification rests not upon what he thinks, but upon the attendant circumstances which prove that he is right; and, if he is mistaken, if the conditions have not warranted the infraction of the fundamental principle of military efficiency,—obedience,—he must take the full consequences of his error, however honest he may have been.

Mahan then went so far as to admit that most officers were incapable of acting according to his ideal: "There is a certain confusion of thought prevalent on this matter, most holding the rule of obedience too abso-

---

[65] Ibid., 312.
[66] Mahan, *Influence of Sea Power upon History*, 381.
[67] Mahan, *French Revolution and Empire*, i: 205. See also 229, 373; and Mahan, *Nelson*, ii: 327.
[68] Mahan, *Nelson*, i: 84.
[69] Ibid., 190. See also 297.

lutely, others tending to the disorganizing view that the integrity of the
intention is sufficient; the practical result and for the average man the
better result, being to shun the grave responsibility of departing from
the letter of the order."[70]

Indeed, for Mahan, there was much to be said for obedience and discipline as the building blocks of mutual trust and effective cooperation
that were essential to military efficiency—and thus an important naval
professional quality, if less difficult to produce than executive judgment.
In the great four-day battle of June 1666 between the English and
Dutch fleets, the former were beaten badly by the latter. Mahan noted,
however, that the consequences of defeat "would have been much
worse but for the high spirit and skill" with which the plans of the English commander "were carried out by his subordinates, and of the lack
of similar support" in the case of his opponent. Mahan attributed the
English advantage in this respect to their officers' having been im-
planted with "correct military feeling, pride, and discipline."[71] He also
noted with approval that these characteristics existed in part because, at
the time, ships were often commanded by army officers, which meant
that ship handling was entrusted to someone other than the captain,
producing a condition in which there was "a clean division between the
direction of the fighting and of the motive power of the ship."[72]

Having made his positive point, Mahan went on to lament that in the
course of blending the two functions and placing them in the hands of
a single officer, a step that he conceded was necessary for the sake of efficiency and convenience, the

> less important function was allowed to get the upper hand; the
> naval officer came to feel more proud of his dexterity in manag-
> ing the motive power of his ship than of his skill in developing
> her military efficiency. The bad effects of this lack of interest in
> military science became most evident when the point of handling
> fleets was reached, because for that military skill told most, and
> previous study was most necessary; but it was felt in the single
> ship as well. Hence it came to pass, and especially in the English
> navy, that the pride of the seaman took the place of the pride of
> the military man. The English naval officer thought more of that

[70] Ibid., 190–1.
[71] Mahan, *Influence of Sea Power upon History*, 126.
[72] Ibid., 127.

which likened him to the merchant captain than of that which made him akin to the soldier.[73]

Mahan then observed that this did not occur in the French navy and that even "to this day the same tendency obtains; the direction of the motive power has no such consideration as the military functions in the navies of the Latin nations."[74] The superiority of French over British military qualities, he argued, was such that in the American Revolutionary War,

> men who were first of all military men, inferior though they were in opportunities as seamen to their enemies, could meet them on more than equal terms as to tactical skill, and were practically their superiors in handling fleets. The false theory has already been pointed out, which directed the action of the French fleet not to crushing its enemy, but to some ulterior aim; but this does not affect the fact that in tactical skill the military men were superior to the mere seamen, though their tactical skill was applied to mistaken strategic ends.[75]

The military character of French naval leadership was destroyed during the French Revolution, the explanation of which gave Mahan another opportunity to present his views on the importance of leadership as opposed to matériel. Leadership was the critical factor, he argued, because of the difficulty of the tasks that navies had to perform and the complexity of the institution that was needed to accomplish them:

> Here . . . are to be considered questions of discipline and organization; of the adaptation of means to ends; of the recognition, not only of the possibilities, but also of the limitations, by the nature of the case, by the element in which it moves, by the force to which it owes its motion, by the skill or lack of skill with which its powers are used and its deficiencies compensated. . . . The yoke of military service sits hard on those who do not always bear it. Yet the efficiency of the military sea-officer depended upon his fitness to do these things well because they had been so wrought into his own personal habits as to become a second nature.

---

[73] Ibid., 127–8.
[74] Ibid., 128.
[75] Ibid., 129.

This was true, abundantly true, of the single ship in fight; but when it came to the question of combining the force of a great many guns, mounted on perhaps twenty-five or thirty heavy ships, possessing unequal qualities, but which must nevertheless keep close to one another, in certain specified positions, on dark nights, in bad weather, above all when before the enemy; when these ships were called upon to perform evolutions altogether, or in succession, to concentrate upon a part of the enemy, to frustrate by well combined and well executed movements attacks upon themselves, to remedy the inconvenience arising from loss of sails and masts and consequent loss of motive power, to provide against the disorders caused by sudden changes of wind and various chances of the sea—under these conditions, even one not having the knowledge of experience begins to see that such demands can only be met by a body of men of special aptitudes and training, such as in fact has rarely, if ever, been found in perfection, in even the most highly organized fleets of any navy in the world.[76]

"Historically, good men with poor ships," Mahan argued, "are better than poor men with good ships; over and over again the French Revolution taught this lesson, which our own age, with its rage for the last new thing in material improvement, has largely dropped out of memory."[77] The naval superiority of Great Britain in the age of Nelson, Mahan later observed, "lay not in the number of her ships, but in the wisdom, energy, and tenacity of her admirals and seamen."[78] Mahan granted that the advent of steam propulsion—by reducing the difficulties and uncertainties of movement—had diminished the value of the human element,[79] but he remained convinced that it was still more important than technical factors. Constant "production and development of material," he wrote about his own time, was a necessary part of a great nation "endeavoring to maintain its place in the naval scale" in peace, but in the event of war, the main object of policy would be "to put an end to a period of national tension and expense by destroying the enemy."[80] This could be accomplished only with skilled seamen and effective commanders.

---

[76] Mahan, *French Revolution and Empire*, i: 38, 40–1.
[77] Ibid., i: 102.
[78] Mahan, *French Revolution and Empire*, ii: 141.
[79] Ibid. See also Mahan, *Nelson*, i: 226.
[80] Mahan, *1812*, ii: 52.

CHAPTER FOUR

Strategic and Professional Argument in the Lesser Works

Words do not express things;
Phrases do not show the mind movement.
He who receives (only) words is lost;
To stagnate with sentences is to be deluded.

—Mumon Ekai, *Mumonkan* (*The Gateless Gate*)

The intellect is always indirect in its relation to life, it is a generalizing agency, and what is general is lacking in instinctive force, that is, in will-power.

—D. T. Suzuki, "Painting, Swordsmanship, Tea Ceremony"

BIOGRAPHY AS POLEMIC

The first of Mahan's lesser works was a biography of the American Civil War naval leader and hero Admiral David Glasgow Farragut. Unlike any of the other naval books written after *The Gulf and Island Waters*, *Admiral Farragut* focused upon events in which the main action was in America and both antagonists were American. The operational history portions, which made up nearly two-thirds of the text, recovered much of the ground traced in Mahan's first book. Most of the information about Farragut's personal and professional life was drawn from a pre-existing biography written by his son. This relieved Mahan of the hard spadework in primary sources that was the hallmark of the Nelson biography (the publication of which followed shortly after the biography of Farragut) and the later volumes on the War of 1812. Backward-looking in terms of both subject and technique, *Admiral Farragut* requires treatment separate from that of its fellows.

In this book, Mahan touched upon the large geopolitical themes characteristic of the "Influence of Sea Power" series, as he had in *The Gulf and Inland Waters*.[1] He also had occasion to amplify his earlier analysis of riverine and littoral warfare, showing a keen appreciation of its peculiarities and of the desirability and even necessity of cordial co-operation between the army and navy.[2] Although these subjects would never again receive his serious attention and cannot be considered an integral part of the exposition of his grand historical view of sea power, *Admiral Farragut* reveals Mahan's substantial understanding of maritime "little war," an understanding, it should be remembered, that was based upon wartime experience, personal knowledge of many of the participants in the events described, and serious scholarship.

The main connection between *Admiral Farragut* and Mahan's other work is to be found in his presentation of the major elements of his professional argument, which was the principal subtext of the biography. Mahan believed that certain authors had placed too much emphasis upon aggressive spirit as the basis of successful military leadership. He thus took pains to point out that Farragut's daring "was guided by a calculation of the comparative *material* risks and advantages" and not mere bluff aimed at the enemy's morale. "The serious objection to relying upon moral effect alone to overcome resistance," Mahan argued, was that

> . . . moral forces do not admit of as close knowledge and measurement as do material conditions. The insight and moral strength of the enemy may be greater than you have means of knowing, and to assume that they are less is to fall into the dangerous error of despising your enemy. To attribute to so dubious a hope, alone, the daring act of Admiral Farragut in passing the forts and encountering the imperfectly known dangers above, is really to detract from his fame as a capable as well as gallant leader. That there were risks and accidents to be met he knew

---

[1] Captain A. T. Mahan, *Admiral Farragut* (New York: D. Appleton, 1892), 6, 7, 19, 115–7, 176, 242.
[2] See especially ibid., 206.

full well; that he might incur disaster he realized; that the dangers above and the power of the enemy's vessels might exceed his expectations was possible; war can not be stripped of hazard, and the anxiety of the doubtful issue is the penalty the chieftain pays for his position.[3]

Mahan, in his examination of Farragut's riverine operations of 1862 and 1863, contrasted the caution displayed by the Union officer when basic conditions were unfavorable to the point of precluding action with his willingness to advance when changed circumstances justified a different course:

> To push far up a narrow and intricate river a force of ships whose numbers are insufficient even to protect their own communications and insure their coal supplies, is one thing; it is quite another to repair to the same scene of action prepared to support the army by controlling the water, and by establishing in combined action a secure secondary base of operations from which further advances can be made with reasonable certainty of holding the ground gained. There was no inconsistency between Farragut's reluctance of the spring and his forwardness in the autumn.[4]

During the operations of the fall, which were conducted against great adversity and involved heavy losses, Farragut's resolution saved the day. Mahan believed this case offered "a consummate example of professional conduct."[5] He also attributed the decision to launch the campaign in the face of significant risks, which was justified by its ultimate success, to Farragut's ability to separate "a clear appreciation of facts from a confused impression of possibilities."[6]

Mahan did not, however, discount the importance of daring. Nelson, he noted, laid heavy emphasis upon the importance of "direct, rapid, and vigorous action without which no military operations, however wisely planned, can succeed. In the want of this, rather than of great professional acquirements, will be most frequently found the difference between the successful and the unsuccessful general; and consequently

---

[3] Ibid., 143–4. Italics in the original.
[4] Ibid., 199–200.
[5] Ibid., 216.
[6] Ibid., 232.

Nelson, who had seen so much of failure arising from slowness and over-caution, placed, and rightly placed, more stress upon vigor and rapidity, in which most are found deficient, than upon the methods which many understand, however ill they may apply them."[7] Daring had to be combined with tenacity and a willingness to assume responsibility. "The acquirements of the accomplished officer," Mahan warned,

> may enable him to see the right thing to be done under given conditions, and yet fail to lift him to the height of due performance. It is in the strength of purpose, in the power of rapid decision, of instant action, and, if need be, of strenuous endurance through a period of danger or of responsibility, when the terrifying alternatives of war are vibrating in the balance, that the power of a great captain mainly lies. It is in the courage to apply knowledge under conditions of exceptional danger; not merely to see the true direction for effort to take, but to dare to follow it, accepting all the risks and all the chances inseparable from war, facing all that defeat means in order thereby to secure victory if it may be had.[8]

Having delineated the qualities required of an effective commander, Mahan did not shy from the task of criticizing educational practices that he believed interfered with their growth. The "idea of professional improvement in the United States Navy," he argued,

> has fastened . . . upon the development of the material of war, to the comparative exclusion of the study of naval warfare. This naturally results from the national policy, which does not propose to put afloat a fleet in the proper sense of the word; and whose ideal is a number more or less small, of cruisers neither fitted nor intended for combined action. Under these circumstances, the details of the internal economy of the single ship usurp in the professional mind an undue proportion of the attention which, in a rightly constituted navy, might far better be applied to the study of naval tactics, in the higher sense of that word, and of naval campaigns.[9]

---

[7] Ibid., 309–10.
[8] Ibid., 317. See also 318.
[9] Ibid., 314.

Farragut himself, Mahan observed, recognized that "the rage for material advance, though a good thing, carries with it the countervailing disposition to rely upon perfected material rather than upon accomplished warriors to decide the issue of battle," and that his misgivings were those of "a born master of war, who feels, even without reasoning, that men are always prone to rely upon instruments rather than upon living agents—to think the armor greater than the man."[10]

In September 1894, some two years after the publication of *Admiral Farragut*, Mahan conceded to an English critic that he perhaps had gone "too far to my own extreme of exalting the Art of War, in its various branches, over the absorbing attention to matériel on the part of naval officers of the executive branch." He also at this time declined a commission offered by his correspondent to redress the imbalance in a paper, offering the excuse that he was "a slow, meditative kind of writer, perfectly incapable of dashing off my ideas on such a subject, or even of saying with precision just what my ideas are. While my mind is reasonably active and fruitful, it deliberately refuses to be "bossed"; and when tired out with the details of ship economy it strikes work and can be neither persuaded nor bullied into action."[11] Mahan's mention of "the details of ship economy" referred to the labors associated with his command of the cruiser U.S.S. *Chicago*. His retirement from active service in 1896, however, allowed him not only to produce the final installment of the "Influence of Sea Power" series but to write articles about a wide range of subjects.

CRITIQUE OF ENGINEERING
AND ADMINISTRATIVE MINDSETS

Mahan's first collection of short pieces, titled *The Interest of America in Sea Power, Present and Future*, which appeared in 1897, was a disparate lot. Most of the articles in it had been written before his taking leave of the navy. "If such unity perchance be found in these," he wrote in the preface, "it will not be due to antecedent purpose, but to the fact that they embody the thought of an individual mind, consecutive in the line

---

[10] Ibid., 324.
[11] Mahan to Admiral Cyprian A. G. Bridge, 18 September 1894, in *The Letters and Papers of Alfred Thayer Mahan*, ed. Robert Seager II and Doris Maguire, 3 vols. (Annapolis, Md.: Naval Institute Press, 1975), ii: 332 (hereinafter cited as *LPATM*).

of its main conceptions, but adjusting itself continually to changing conditions, which the progress of events entails."[12] The foregoing remarks are more or less applicable to all the post–*Admiral Farragut* lesser works considered as a whole.[13] Book-by-book treatment would fragment analysis to little purpose. Examination of this material will thus be thematic, with two of the five kinds of Mahanian argument being considered: professional and strategic. Treatment of the first, second, and third forms of argument—that is, political, political-economic, and governmental argument (the first two in terms of late-nineteenth- and twentieth-century conditions)—is reserved for the next chapter. To avoid awkward repetition, only the original publication dates of quoted passages are given, with complete identification left to the notes.

For Mahan, the essence of effective naval executive attitude was to be found in judicious risk-taking, which he regarded as the antithesis of rigidly cautious decision-making mind-sets formed by technical or administrative experience. In 1888, Mahan argued that segregating the study of war from the "mechanical and material advance" that defined "the spirit of our age" was required to counteract the "effect of that spirit upon our naval officers."[14] In war, he observed in 1899, "failure to dare is often to run the greatest of risks," and a man was "unfit for command" who was "unable to run a very great risk for the sake of decisive advantage."[15] In 1902, Mahan insisted that chance, the unexpected, and risk were "inseparable from war" and constituted as "much of its opportunity as of its danger."[16] In 1907, he noted that "men are greater than ships," and that in matters of naval officer education he had

[12] Captain A. T. Mahan, *The Interest of America in Sea Power, Present and Future* (Boston: Little, Brown, 1897), v.

[13] Mahan produced seven anthologies of articles, a biography, an autobiography, a volume of his collected Naval War College lectures, two book-length essays on international relations, an account of the Boer War, a theological monograph, and a survey history of naval operations during the American Revolution. A chronological listing in standard form is given in the bibliography.

[14] A. T. Mahan, "Objects of the United States Naval War College," address, August 1888, reprinted in Captain A. T. Mahan, *Naval Administration and Warfare: Some General Principles with Other Essays* (Boston: Little, Brown, 1908), 187. See also 188.

[15] "Lessons of the War with Spain, 1898" (I, V), *McClure's Magazine* (December 1898, April 1899), reprinted in Alfred T. Mahan, *Lessons of the War with Spain and Other Articles* (Boston: Little Brown, 1899), 23, 190.

[16] "Considerations Governing the Disposition of Navies," *National Review* (July 1902), reprinted in A. T. Mahan, *Retrospect and Prospect: Studies in International Relations Naval and Political* (London: Sampson Low, Marston, 1902), 193. See also A.T. Mahan, *Naval Strategy* (Boston: Little, Brown, 1911), 430–1; and A. T. Mahan, *The Major Operations of the Navies in the War of American Independence* (Boston: Little, Brown, 1913), 104, 173–4, 223.

"sympathized in the main with those who would subordinate the technological element to the more strictly professional."[17]

Mahan's animus against his service's tendency to favor engineering expertise in policy matters was reflected in his views on naval architecture. In 1898, he declared that the design of warships was not a technical but a military question[18] and provided a list of his basic principles of warship design. In essence, these reflected his view that concentration of force was best expressed in the possession of a large number of moderate-sized battleships rather than a smaller number of more powerful units.[19] Mahan also gave this opinion in articles about the conflict between Russia and Japan, published in May and June 1906.[20] In addition, Mahan pointed out that increasing size brought commensurate increases in cost, which had serious political implications.[21] By this date, however, a wide range of financial, technical, tactical, and strategic developments had prompted the British Admiralty to order the construction of new-model capital ships of unprecedented dimensions, speed, and firepower.[22] The first units came into service between 1906 and

---

[17] Captain A. T. Mahan, *From Sail to Steam: Recollections of Naval Life* (New York: Harper and Brothers, 1907), 25, 45.

[18] "Distinguishing Qualities of Ships of War," Scripps-McRae Newspaper League (November 1898), reprinted in Mahan, *Lessons of the War with Spain*, 257. For Mahan on the priority of military over engineering or administrative considerations in warships design, see also A. T. Mahan, *Types of Naval Officers Drawn from the History of the British Navy* (Boston: Little, Brown, 1901), 19; Mahan to Washington I. Chambers, 27 July 1892, *LPATM*, ii: 75–7; Mahan to John D. Long, 31 January 1900, *LPATM*, ii: 680–1; Mahan to Theodore Roosevelt, 16 October 1902 and 7 September 1903, *LPATM*, iii: 38–40, 74; and Mahan to William H. Moody, 1 February 1909, *LPATM*, iii: 280–1. For Mahan's opposition to the call for an increase in the influence of naval engineers in matters of naval policy, see Mahan to the editor of the *New York Times*, 28 October 1897, *LPATM*, ii: 528.

[19] Ibid., 260–9. See also Mahan to the editor of the *New York Sun*, 9 May 1904, *LPATM*, iii: 90–5. For Mahan's reservations about big guns, based on his long experience with nineteenth-century ordnance, see Mahan to Washington C. Whitthorne, 21 March 1876, *LPATM*, i: 448–9.

[20] A.T. Mahan, "Retrospect upon the War between Japan and Russia," *National Review* (May 1906), reprinted in Mahan, *Naval Administration and Warfare*; and A.T. Mahan, "Reflections, Historic and Others, Suggested by the Battle of the Sea of Japan," *U.S. Naval Institute Proceedings* (June 1906).

[21] Mahan, "Retrospect upon the War between Japan and Russia," 142. For Mahan's belief that the introduction of warships of ever-increasing size and the consequent discarding of superseded but still new units would lead to financial crisis and the suspension of naval preparation, see Mahan to William H. Henderson, 16 February 1909 and 17 May 1910, *LPATM*, iii: 285, 342. These considerations appear to have overcome his belief that one large warship was superior in fighting power to several smaller units of greater aggregate force, for which see Captain A. T. Mahan, *The Influence of Sea Power upon the French Revolution and Empire, 1793–1812*, 2 vols. (Boston: Little, Brown, 1892), i: 128.

[22] Jon Tetsuro Sumida, *In Defence of Naval Supremacy: Finance, Technology and British Naval Policy, 1889–1914* (Boston: Unwin Hyman, 1989).

1908, establishing an international standard that was emulated by every first- and second-class naval power. Mahan's arguments were thus widely dismissed as technically passé and thus irrelevant.[23]

Mahan, for the most part, abandoned writing on naval architecture. While he was not convinced completely that his critics were right, he did not republish the more technical article on the Russo-Japanese War in any of his hardcover collections, and much of the technical commentary in the second piece was cut when it was anthologized.[24] His autobiography, which was written at the time of his involvement in the controversy over capital ship design, closed on a dispirited note: "I know too well that, when you come to details, prediction is a matter of hit or miss, and that I have often missed as well as hit in particulars." Mahan then observed that he could recognize in himself, at the age of sixty-seven, "a growing conservatism, which may probably limit me henceforth to bare [*sic*] keeping up with the procession in the future national march" and conceded that "perhaps I may lag behind."[25] In subsequent books, the subject of warship design was largely avoided.[26]

Technological change aside, the creation and maintenance of a large fleet of up-to-date warships posed complex administrative problems. In Mahan's account of the wars of the French Revolution and Empire, he had recognized that much of British success in the war at sea was attributable to strong administration and that French failure was at bottom a matter of major shortcomings in this area.[27] In his occasional writing, however, Mahan dichotomized warfare and administration, presenting them as conflicting in spirit, if not in interest. He wrote in 1903,

> Naval administration, in the common acceptation of the term, is mostly office work. It comes into contact with the Navy proper chiefly through official correspondence, less by personal inter-

---

[23] Robert Seager II, *Alfred Thayer Mahan: The Man and His Letters* (Annapolis, Md.: Naval Institute Press, 1977), 518–35 (hereinafter cited as *ATM*).

[24] Mahan, *Naval Administration and Warfare*, x–xi.

[25] Mahan, *From Sail to Steam*, 326. For Mahan's reluctance to engage tactical and technical questions as such, see Mahan to Theodore Roosevelt, 8 October 1906, *LPATM*, iii: 178–80; Mahan to William H. Henderson, 19 January 1907, *LPATM*, iii: 204; and Mahan to William H. Henderson, 17 May 1910, *LPATM*, iii: 342. Published criticism then prompted private rebuttal, for which see Mahan to Theodore Roosevelt, 22 October 1906, *LPATM*, iii: 182–9.

[26] For the exceptions, see A. T. Mahan, *Naval Strategy* (Boston: Little, Brown, 1911), 44, 390–1; and A. T. Mahan, *Armaments and Arbitration, or the Place of Force in the International Relations of States* (New York: Harper, 1912), 18–9.

[27] Mahan, *French Revolution and Empire*, i: 68, 96.

course with the officers concerned; still less by immediate contact with the daily life of the profession, which it learns at second hand. It consequently tends to overvalue the orderly routine and observance of the system by which it receives information, transmits orders, checks expenditure, files returns, and, in general, keeps with the service the touch of paper; in short, the organization which has been created for facilitating its own labours. In due measure these are imperatively necessary; but it is undeniable that the practical tendency is to exaggerate their importance relatively to the executive end proposed.[28]

Mahan's fundamental complaint was not with administration as such, but with bureaucratization. And even bureaucracy, he recognized, was necessary because the multiplicity of complex tasks required a division of labor. The great drawback was that distributed work partitioned responsibility, a division that Mahan believed was antithetical to sound— that is, intelligent, rapid, and unequivocal—decision-making.[29] He was nevertheless resigned to the fact that maintenance of a balance between the needs of administration and of warfare was unavoidable. "The two great oppositions," he wrote in 1903, ". . . —civil versus military, unity of action against multiplicity of activities—are but a reflection of the essential problem of warfare. A saying has been attributed by [French politician and historian Louis-Adolphe] Thiers to the great Napoleon, that the difficulty of the Art of War consists in concentrating in order to fight, and disseminating in order to subsist. There is no other, he said, aphoristically. The problem is one of embracing opposites."[30]

These opposing activities, Mahan argued elsewhere, did not exclude each other, but there was "between them the relation of greater and less."[31] Moreover, while Mahan believed that administration was most

[28] A. T. Mahan, "Principles of Naval Administration: American and British Systems Compared," *National Review* (June 1903), reprinted in Mahan, *Naval Administration and Warfare*, 9–10.
[29] Mahan to Washington I. Chambers, 27 July 1892, *LPATM*, ii: 75; Mahan to John M. Brown, 1 June 1893, *LPATM*, ii: 109; Mahan to John D. Long, 10 May and 14 September 1898, *LPATM*, ii: 551–2, 594–5; Mahan to Stephen B. Luce, 31 August 1898, *LPATM*, ii: 592.
[30] Mahan, "Principles of Naval Administration," 20. Mahan's views on the necessity of dividing the workload of administration were long-held. See Mahan to Samuel A. Ashe, 12 March 1880, *LPATM*, i: 481–2. For Mahan's personal familiarity with the drudgery of routine administration, see Mahan to John H. Upshur, 2 and 3 October 1882, *LPATM*, i: 536–7.
[31] Mahan, "Principles of Naval Administration," 9.

efficient when "in peace the contingency of war has dictated its system,"[32] he did not hold with its reciprocal, namely, that the direction of war needed to be informed by an appreciation of administrative imperatives. "In military activities," he maintained in 1911,

> the question of the utilization of the armed forces is the most
> critical and the most vital that confronts a nation. . . . Utilization
> presupposes all the successive processes of organization and
> equipment; whereby, step by step, out of individual men are built
> up huge military units, army and army corps, battle-fleet and
> battle-ship. . . . Thus, assuming the foundation upon which action rests, the directing authority dismisses them out of mind,
> concentrating attention purely upon the problem how best *to use*
> those entities which organization and equipment have supplied.[33]

The effect of giving the use of military power such absolute priority over and independence from the sources of that power was compounded by Mahan's reluctance to write about a subject that he believed was unappetizing to the lay reader. "Administrative details," he observed in 1901, "are interesting only to specialists."[34]

Mahan's tendency to slight naval administration, when combined with his belief that naval officers should avoid "dissipating" energy on thinking about "questions financial, sociological, economical, or what not,"[35] may explain partly his blindness to the growing political-economic importance of warship procurement. In *The Influence of Sea Power upon History*, Mahan observed that "in a representative government any military expenditure must have a strongly represented interest behind it, convinced of its necessity."[36] But the only powerful interest relevant to naval expansion that Mahan recognized was the existence of a large overseas commerce. When confronted by the combination of its absence and substantial naval development in the cases of Russia and the United States, he was compelled to admit that navies could be called

---

[32] Ibid., 8.

[33] Mahan, *Naval Strategy*, 196. Italics in the original.

[34] Mahan, *Types of Naval Officers*, 130. See also 336. For the criticism of the editor of *Scribner's Magazine* of Mahan's article "Principles of Naval Administration: American and British Systems Compared" as too "academic," see Mahan to Leopold Maxse, 28 April 1903, *LPATM*, iii: 60.

[35] Mahan, *Naval Strategy*, 21.

[36] Alfred Thayer Mahan, *The Influence of Sea Power upon History, 1660–1783* (Boston: Little, Brown, 1890), 88. See also 26, 39, 49, 82.

forth by external necessities alone. Mahan never considered the implications of large-scale government purchases of industrial output, in spite of the fact that the formation of what was later to become known as the military-industrial complex was in his day well underway.[37]

PRINCIPLES OF STRATEGY AND THEIR FUNCTIONS

In his lesser works, Mahan clarified the presentation of his strategic argument by explaining that it had two different forms. His basic approach, which was to state fundamental principles and illustrate them with examples, was aimed at naval professionals just beginning their study of strategy and at the intelligent portion of the electorate, whose equipment with even rudimentary knowledge might improve their capacity to choose or support competent government.[38] This "effort to co-ordinate the data, to point out their significance, to elicit their teaching, and to formulate it into principles or definitions," he noted in 1911, amounted to an "attempt at systematizing."[39] Mahan's more advanced method, which was to provide a detailed narrative of operations accompanied by sophisticated analysis, was meant for those who had mastered the basics and were prepared for harder and more extended labor—mainly naval officers, political leaders, and serious thinkers of any stripe.[40] Here, as Mahan explained in 1907, his "critical analysis of the naval campaigns and battles" was "not formal, nor systematic."[41]

---

[37] Mahan's views of administration in the early twentieth century seem to have been based upon his experience in administration a quarter-century earlier, when warship procurement was hardly an issue. See Mahan to George H. Cooper, 13 January 1882, *LPATM*, i: 513–5. For Mahan's dislike of the influence of political considerations on the selection of locations for naval bases, see Mahan to Robert U. Johnson, 26 December 1910, *LPATM*, iii: 369. For the formation of the military-industrial complex in America, see Benjamin Franklin Cooling, *Gray Steel and Blue Water Navy: The Formative Years of America's Military-Industrial Complex, 1881–1917* (Hamden, Conn.: Archon, 1979); and Thomas J. Misa, *A Nation of Steel: The Making of Modern America, 1865–1925* (Baltimore, Md.: Johns Hopkins University Press, 1995), chap. 3.
[38] Mahan, "Lessons of the War with Spain, 1898" (Introductory), 6–7, 10–11, 14; A. T. Mahan, "Principles Involved in the War between Japan and Russia," *National Review* (September 1904), and "Subordination in Historical Treatment," address to the American Historical Association, December 1902, both reprinted in Mahan, *Naval Administration and Warfare*, 94, 95, 251–2. See also Mahan to Little, Brown, 6 June 1908, *LPATM*, iii: 249.
[39] Mahan, *Naval Strategy*, 112.
[40] Mahan, "Lessons of the War with Spain, 1898" (Introductory), 7–10.
[41] Mahan, *From Sail to Steam*, 283. For Mahan's revealing criticism of a work of Julian Corbett, the well-known British naval historian, as excessively theoretical, see Mahan to John P. Merrell, 20 December 1908, *LPATM*, iii: 273.

Mahan believed that strategic principles were the embodiment of "fundamental truth,"[42] that history could be used as testimony to their validity, and that the two combined were "a perfect instructor."[43] "Master your principles," he declared, "and then ram them home with the illustrations which History furnishes."[44] On the other hand, Mahan did not believe that "fundamental truth" was the whole or even most of the truth, nor that "a perfect instructor" answered all necessities. In 1888, he made a distinction between "cast-iron rules of invariable application" and "general principles" that were adaptable to "ever-shifting circumstances."[45] In 1899, Mahan could allow the possibility of conditions commanding the "non-observance" of even a "well-founded and generally accepted principle of war."[46] In 1907, he wrote that principles were not "pedantic precedents."[47] In 1911, Mahan observed that although "sound military principle is as useful to military conduct as moral principle is to integrity in life," the "application of a principle to a particular case is often difficult, in war or in morals."[48] And in 1912, he noted that "a principle is essentially a generality" and that it was therefore "in the application of it to a concrete case that the difficulty lies."[49]

Mahan recognized that the formulation of a system of principles and the dissemination of the resulting doctrine—which were important aspects of the work of war colleges—were required to ensure effective command in war. The imposition of a common set of action principles, he argued in 1911, meant that "within a pretty wide range there will be in a school of officers a certain homogeneousness of intellectual equipment and conviction which will tend to cause likeness of impulse and of conduct under any set of given conditions. The formation of a similar habit of thought, and of assurance as to the right thing to do under particular circumstances, reinforces strongly the power of co-operation, which is the essential factor in military operations."[50] But Mahan was

---

[42] Mahan, *Naval Strategy*, 2.

[43] Ibid., 17.

[44] Ibid.

[45] Mahan, "Objects of the United States Naval War College," 191.

[46] Mahan, "Lessons of the War with Spain, 1898" (IV), 168. See also 170.

[47] Mahan, *From Sail to Steam*, 282. See also "Objects of the United States Naval War College," 191.

[48] Mahan, *Naval Strategy*, 234. See also 2, 115, 240, 300, 429.

[49] Mahan, *Armaments and Arbitration*, 68. See also "Lessons of the War with Spain, 1898" (IV), 168; and Mahan to Raymond P. Rodgers, 4 March 1911, *LPATM*, iii: 394.

[50] Mahan, *Naval Strategy*, 201.

conscious of the tendency of doctrine to interfere with the exercise of intelligent judgment, which to him was also of critical importance. "The French word *doctrinaire*, fully adopted into English," he thus wrote, "gives warning of the danger that attends doctrine; a danger to which all useful conceptions are liable," which was the propensity to exaggerate "the letter above the spirit, of becoming mechanical instead of discriminating."[51]

For Mahan, principles and doctrine were beneficial insofar as they facilitated further learning, a degree of understanding, or cooperation in action; they were harmful when they acted in place of the exercise of flexible intelligence. War, he wrote in 1899, "is a matter, not merely of knowledge and of general principles, but of sound judgment without which both information and rules, being wrongly applied, become useless."[52] Mahan believed that such a capacity for good decision-making could be improved through the study of detailed and critical history, which had "no limit short of the military experience of the race," recording "the effect of moral influences of every kind, as well as of the most diverse material conditions."[53] Officers who had received proper historical training, Mahan was convinced, would be able to learn from direct experience more quickly than those who had not. Thus he argued that serious understanding of the past would not produce a fruit "fully matured" but one that nonetheless achieved a "perfection of form which requires but a few suns to ripen."[54]

Mahan restated these views more than a decade later in 1911 in even stronger and more comprehensive terms:

> It is in the application of sound general principles to particular problems of war that difficulty arises. The principles are few, the cases very various, the smaller details almost infinitely numerous. Here experience enters—experience which, under the form of the word *experiments*, lies at the basis of all our science. But how shall experience of war be acquired in the absence of a state of war? And even amid constant war, how shall any one man, particularly

---

[51] Ibid., 204. Italics in the original. On the dangers of doctrine and rigidity in application, see also Mahan to George Sydenham Clarke, 30 September 1894, *LPATM*, ii: 337–8, and Mahan, *The Major Operations of the Navies*, 146.
[52] Mahan, "Lessons of the War with Spain, 1898" (Introductory), 10.
[53] Ibid., 8.
[54] Ibid.

a subaltern or naval captain, find in his own experience all, or any
large portion of the innumerable cases that may and do arise? No
one will answer that he can so find them.[55]

"There is yet another and deeper thought," Mahan continued later,

> underlying the advice to study the campaigns of great comman-
> ders. It is not merely that the things they have done become a
> catalogue of precedents, to which a well stored memory can refer
> as special cases arise for decision. Such a mechanical employment
> of them has its advantage, can be consigned to treatises, and can
> be usefully taught to those who will learn nothing otherwise. But,
> beyond and above this, it is by that diligent study which Napo-
> leon enjoins that the officer who so lives with these men absorbs
> not merely the dry practice, but the spirit and understanding
> which filled and guided them. There is such a thing as becoming
> imbued with the spirit of a great teacher, as well as acquainted
> with his maxims.[56]

Mahan then described proper operational practice as an art rather
than a science:

> Science is sure of nothing until it is proved; but, all the same, it
> aims at absolute certainties,—dogmas,—towards which, through
> numerous experiments, it keeps moving. Its truths, once estab-
> lished, are fixed, rigid, unbending, and the relation between cause
> and effect are rather laws than principles; hard lines incapable of
> change, rather than living seeds. Science discovers and teaches
> truths which it has no power to change; Art, out of materials
> which it finds about it, creates new forms in endless variety. It is
> not bound down to a mechanical reproduction of similar effects,
> as is inanimate nature, but partakes of the freedom of the human
> mind in which it has its root. Art acknowledges principles and
> even rules; but these are not so much fetters, or bars, which com-
> pel its movements aright, as guides which warn when it is going
> wrong. In this living sense, the conduct of war is an art, having its
> spring in the mind of man, dealing with very various circum-

---

[55] Mahan, *Naval Strategy*, 297. Italics in the original.
[56] Ibid., 298. See also 9–10.

stances, admitting certain principles; but, beyond that, manifold in its manifestations, according to the genius of the artist and the temper of the materials with which he is dealing. . . .

Maxims of war, therefore, are not so much positive rules as they are the developments and applications of a few general principles. They resemble the ever varying, yet essentially like, forms that spring from living seeds, rather than the rigid framework to which the free growth of a plant is sometimes forced to bend itself. . . .

The maxim, rooting itself in a principle, formulates a rule generally correct under the conditions; but the teacher must admit that each case has its own features—like the endless variety of the one human face—which modify the application of the rule, and may even make it at times wholly inapplicable. It is for the skill of the artist in war rightly to apply the principles and rules in each case.[57]

CLOSE REASONING AND QUALIFICATION

"In studying warfare," Mahan declared in 1911, "as in every other subject, do not despise words, nor be indifferent to the precision and fullness of their meaning."[58] In his autobiography, he had confessed that "the besetting anxiety of my soul was to be exact and lucid," which meant that "to be accurate in facts and correct in conclusions, both as to appreciation and expression, dominated all other motives."[59] The consequence of his acting upon this impulse was, if not a surfeit of fact, a habit of close reasoning that he himself recognized was not easy to follow. He went on to admit,

> The aim to be thus both accurate and clear often encumbered my sentences. My cautious mind strove to introduce between the same two periods every qualification, whether in abatement or enforcement of the leading idea or statement. This in many cases meant an accumulation of clauses, over which I exercised my ingenuity and lavished my time so to arrange them that the whole should be at once apprehended by the reader. It was not enough

[57] Ibid., 299–300.
[58] Ibid., 389.
[59] Mahan, *From Sail to Steam*, 288.

for me that the qualifications should appear a page or two before, or after, and in this I think myself right; but in wanting them all in the same period, as I instinctively did,—and do, for nature is obstinate,—I have imposed on myself needless labor, and have often taxed attention as an author has no right to do. . . . It is to this anxiety for full and accurate development of statements and ideas that I chiefly attribute a diffuseness with which my writing has been reproached; I have no doubt justly.[60]

Mahan's propensity to seek accuracy through qualification—which in effect transformed simple statements into complex ones—was exercised frequently in the lesser books when he reconsidered strategic argument that had been put forward in the "Influence of Sea Power" books. In 1894, for example, he tried to qualify his preference for fleets based on battleships as opposed to those based on cruisers by drawing a distinction between *guerre de course* (privateering) and commerce-destroying. He maintained that the two terms were far from equivalent; the former was too weak a form of war to achieve the latter. "It is only when effort is frittered away in the feeble dissemination of the *guerre-de-course*," Mahan explained, "instead of being concentrated in a great combination to control the sea, that commerce-destroying justly incurs the reproach of misdirected effort."[61] Mahan again exposed the American institutional assumptions that underlay his views of the relative merits of building battleships or cruisers by not only deprecating the building of the latter but maintaining in 1898 that "much of the duties of this class . . . can be discharged fairly well by purchased vessels."[62]

Mahan also offered a full explanation of the confusing association of grand-strategic defensive and strategic offensive, which he had advo-

---

[60] Ibid., 288–9.
[61] A. T. Mahan, "Possibilities of an Anglo-American Reunion," *North American Review* (November 1894), reprinted in Mahan, *Interest of America in Sea Power*, 133–4. See also 128–9. For the central role of commerce destruction in Mahan's conception of protracted war, and in particular the equivalency of blockade and commerce-raiding, see A. T. Mahan, "The Hague Conference: The Question of Immunity for Belligerent Merchant Shipping," *National Review* (July 1907), reprinted in A. T. Mahan, *Some Neglected Aspects of War* (Boston: Little, Brown, 1907), 173–4.
[62] Mahan, "Distinguishing Qualities of Ships of War," 273. For the ability of flotilla forces to be formed from inexperienced men, and the more stringent personnel requirements of battle fleets, see A. T. Mahan, "Preparedness for Naval War," *Harper's New Monthly Magazine* (September 1897), reprinted in Mahan, *Interest of America in Sea Power*, 196–7, 202–3, 203, 205; and *Types of Naval Officers*, 291–2, 309. For the mythology of commerce-raiding efficacy in its particularly American form, see Mahan, *From Sail to Steam*, 269–70.

cated previously in the "Influence of Sea Power" series.[63] His main argument was that offensive and defensive actions were complements rather than opposites. The "best and only sure form of defense," he observed in 1902, "is to take the offensive,"[64] adding later that the fundamental principle of maritime war was that "defense is insured only by offense,"[65] and, indeed, that "defense and offense" were "closely identified."[66] "A sound defensive scheme, sustaining the bases of the national force," Mahan also insisted, "is the foundation upon which war rests; but who lays a foundation without intending a superstructure? The offensive element in warfare is the superstructure, the end and aim for which the defensive exists, and apart from which it is to all purposes of war worse than useless."[67] In a similar spirit, Mahan in 1911 accepted as valid Clausewitz's dictum that defense, as compared with offense, was the stronger form of war but went on to add strong qualifications.[68]

Mahan called for both offensive behavior in the performance of defensive function and defense as the prerequisite for offense, in his discussions of coastal defense. In 1898, 1899, and 1911, Mahan again argued that provision of adequate military coastal defenses was necessary to free the battle fleet for offensive action in distant waters.[69] In 1911, he repeated his view that battle fleets were superior to purely local forms of coastal defense as protectors of home maritime interests because of their capacity to act offensively—that is, to be capable of either "driving away or drawing away" enemy naval forces.[70] At this time, he also attempted to reconcile the use of surface torpedo craft and submarines in coastal defense with his offensive principles—and also paved the way for a modification of his strictures against the effectiveness of flotilla craft as instruments of coastal defense—by claiming that "the chief role of the torpedo-vessels is in *attack* upon a hostile fleet which is trying to maintain its ground near the port."[71]

---

[63] Mahan, *Influence of Sea Power upon History*, 416; Mahan, *French Revolution and Empire*, i: 199, 201; and Captain A. T. Mahan, *Sea Power in Its Relations to the War of 1812*, 2 vols. (Boston: Little, Brown, 1905), i: 298.

[64] A. T. Mahan, "Conditions Determining the Naval Expansion of the United States," *Leslie's Weekly* (2 October 1902), reprinted in Mahan, *Retrospect and Prospect*, 40.

[65] Ibid., 168.

[66] Ibid., 163. See also 155–6.

[67] Ibid., 151. See also 153.

[68] Mahan, *Naval Strategy*, 277–80.

[69] Mahan, "Lessons of the War with Spain, 1898" (Introductory, I, II), xii–xiii, 48–50, 63–9; and Mahan, *Naval Strategy*, 433–5.

[70] Mahan, *Naval Strategy*, 248. See also 243, 249.

[71] Ibid., 147. Italics in the original. For Mahan's general views on submarines, see ibid., 3; and Seager, *ATM*, 537.

In the "Influence of Sea Power" series, Mahan made brief references to the critical role played by intelligence in certain important operations during the Napoleonic Wars.[72] In 1899, Mahan went further by formulating the general observation that "accurate intelligence is one of the very first *desiderata* of war."[73] On a different matter, Mahan in 1911 reiterated his dislike for amphibious operations in support of army campaigns when he argued that such actions possessed the advantage of surprise but imposed the burden of maintaining communications. Military attacks from the sea, Mahan argued, were "harder to sustain than to make."[74] Mahan also had much to say about logistics in its own right. In 1901, he observed that sound logistics were essential to the success of Britain's blockade of French ports during the Seven Years' War.[75] In 1907, he went so far as to write that in comparison with Nelson's prodigies of warship husbandry before Trafalgar, the battle itself was "relatively a small matter."[76] In Mahan's 1913 account of the American Revolution, he made much of naval logistics and their effect upon certain operations.[77]

Mahan was also aware of the extent to which the adoption of steam propulsion had complicated logistics because of the absolute necessity of providing for fuel. In 1899, he thus expressed approval of the saying that "the only way to have coal enough is to have too much."[78] In 1911, Mahan argued that while steam propulsion had "given increased certainty and quickness of movement to fleets," it had "also imposed upon them such fetters, by the need of renewing their fuel, that naval enterprises can no longer have the daring, far-reaching sweep that they once had."[79] He also pointed out that the need of modern warships for en-

---

[72] Mahan, *French Revolution and Empire*, i: 305, ii: 157–8; and Captain A. T. Mahan, *The Life of Nelson: The Embodiment of the Sea Power of Great Britain*, (Boston: Little, Brown, 1897), i: 234.

[73] Mahan, "Lessons of the War with Spain" (IV), 142. Italics in the original. See also reference to the importance of hydrographic information in Mahan, *Types of Naval Officers*, 112.

[74] Mahan, *Naval Strategy*, 189. See also 190.

[75] Mahan, *Types of Naval Officers*, 108–9.

[76] A. T. Mahan, "The Value of the Pacific Cruise of the United States Fleet, 1908: Prospect," *Scientific American* (7 December 1907), reprinted in Mahan, *Naval Administration and Warfare*, 321. See also description of Howe's performance in 1778 in Mahan, *The Major Operations of the Navies*, 78.

[77] Mahan, *The Major Operations of the Navies*, 116, 195.

[78] Mahan, "Lessons of the War with Spain" (V), 175. See also A. T. Mahan, "The Value of the Pacific Cruise of the United States Fleet, 1908 (Retrospect)," *Collier's Weekly* (29 August 1908), reprinted in Mahan, *Naval Administration and Warfare*, 336–7, 353.

[79] Mahan, *Naval Strategy*, 381. See also 118–9; and Mahan to George von L. Meyer, 21 April 1911, *LPATM*, iii: 399.

gine repairs meant that the availability of dry docks was of the first importance.[80] In 1908, Mahan's appreciation of the significance of fuel and maintenance prompted him to state that a naval base "may be no less determinative of a naval issue than the fleet itself, because it is essential to its existence."[81] In 1912, on the other hand, Mahan warned that although logistics was "as vital to military success as daily food is to daily work, yet, like food, it is not the work."[82]

In 1898, Mahan stated that battle fleets were "the only really determining elements in naval war."[83] Hard scrutiny reveals a degree of equivocation even here, which he presented in expanded form elsewhere. In 1904, Mahan expressed views that demonstrate that the emphasis he placed on the battle fleet and decisive fleet action was open to considerable interpretation. "There is such a thing as the 'sterile glory' of fighting battles," he wrote with regard to the ongoing Russo-Japanese War, "and still more of running risks, the object of which is not worth the possible loss." Mahan then observed that the Japanese might be best advised to "throw the weight of the destruction of the enemy's squadron upon his torpedo vessels and upon the army" than to chance critical damage to their battle fleet. If "control of the sea" could be "attained equally well by other means," he concluded, "the battle fleet should be preserved as both a political and military factor of the first importance."[84]

In 1911, Mahan discussed the possibility of establishing naval superiority in connection with the capture of foreign territory without a battle in one of several ways. Conquest of certain land areas, he argued, might result in naval superiority by "depriving the enemy of a necessary naval base and perhaps of a considerable part of his ships; more generally it will arise from your fleet being superior in numbers or quality to his." It was the absence of these conditions, he went on to say, that would make battle a necessary prerequisite to the securing of naval superiority: "If decisive naval superiority does not exist, you must get ready to fight

---

[80] Mahan, *Naval Strategy*, 163.

[81] Mahan, "Principles Involved in the War Between Japan and Russia," 128.

[82] Mahan, *Armaments and Arbitration*, 200.

[83] Mahan, "Distinguishing Qualities of Ships of War," 262.

[84] Mahan, "Principles Involved in the War between Japan and Russia," 120–1. For Mahan's observation that the enemy's navy was the "great objective" but only "when a reasonable prospect of destroying it, or any large fraction of it, offers," see Mahan, "Lessons of the War with Spain" (IV), 139. On the other hand, for Mahan's admiration of defeat in battle that produced larger favorable results, see Mahan, *The Major Operations of the Navies*, 25.

a battle at sea, upon the results of which will probably depend the final fate of your new gain."[85] In 1912, Mahan argued that "strategic dispositions" that placed a "superior force in a point of decisive vantage" were "more creditable than the bloodiest of head-on victories."[86]

Mahan's cardinal rule of strategy, concentration of force, was no less subject to qualification. In 1911, Mahan declared that "the one great principle of concentration" enjoyed a "predominance, everywhere, under all conditions and from the nature of things."[87] But he then stated that

> like every sound principle, concentration must be held and applied in the spirit, not in the letter only; exercised with understanding, not merely literally. The essential underlying idea is that of mutual support; that the entire force, however distributed at the moment, is acting in such wise that each part is relieved by the others of a part of its own burden; that it also does the same for them; while the disposition in the allotted stations facilitates also timely concentration in mass. A very considerable separation in space may be consistent with such mutual support.[88]

Mahan further observed that the invention of wireless communications meant that "separations can be much wider than once they were, because steam and electricity make movement more certain and communication more quick than in old times," although he was quick to caution that the condition of mutual support still had to be maintained.[89]

PEDAGOGY OF COMMAND AS THEOLOGY

In 1909, Mahan published *The Harvest Within: Thoughts on the Life of a Christian*, a book of theology that merits special consideration in a study

---

[85] Mahan, *Naval Strategy*, 214.
[86] Mahan, *Armaments and Arbitration*, 64.
[87] Mahan, *Naval Strategy*, 49.
[88] Ibid., 74–5. Mahan presented even broader grounds for qualifying the principle of concentration of force in the specific case of the Russian navy before the Russo-Japanese War. See Mahan to George C. Perkins, 11 January 1911, *LPATM*, iii: 372.
[89] Ibid., 75. See also 330–1. For the drawbacks of the British concentration of their battle fleet in home waters, see A. T. Mahan, *The Interest of America in International Conditions* (Boston: Little, Brown, 1910), 151–2.

of Mahan's writing on navies and naval power for several reasons. In the first place, Mahan's approach to the exposition of his religious views followed that of his studies of naval history. On 7 January 1909, he informed an editor at Little, Brown that the writing of the book had "been governed by a leading idea, similar, in its influence upon the work, to that which guided me in the Sea Power series."[90] Yet Mahan also believed that his book was "literally fragmentary, in origin and in essential characteristics" and that although an attempt had been made to "weave these disconnected thoughts into a coherent whole, presenting a certain sequence of arrangement," that there was "in this nothing of the elaboration which inheres in the word 'system.'"[91]

More importantly, Mahan viewed the true acceptance of Christianity as comparable in nature to an act of critical command decision-making in war because both initiatives had to be undertaken in the face of uncertainty. This, indeed, was his "leading idea." "Evidence which would be quite inadequate to hang a man," Mahan argued,

> or to condemn him to imprisonment, may be sufficient to justify action; nay, to compel action. Life abounds in situations where men must make a choice, must act in one direction or another, upon imperfect information. This, again, is one of the conditions upon which even our common daily life is offered to us. In such cases the decision reached is essentially an act of faith, of belief; of conviction, more or less assured, that the situation, so far as indications go, demands the action (or inaction) taken.
>
> But note that, when such imposed conclusion is reached, there follows often the need of a very high moral exertion, of an act of the will; that, namely, of giving one's self over to be possessed by the decision, to act as though it were certainty. Alternatives and hesitations are to be dismissed out of mind. This is Faith, even when exercised in other than religious matters. It is conspicuously required in military conduct, where the unknown quantities are gravest, most appalling. It is a high military virtue, to which in its perfection few attain; one chief factor in military success or unsuccess.[92]

---

[90] Mahan to James W. McIntyre, 7 January 1909, *LPATM*, iii: 274.
[91] A. T. Mahan, *The Harvest Within: Thoughts on the Life of the Christian* (Boston: Little, Brown, 1910), vi–vii.
[92] Ibid., 24.

For Mahan, the mechanism of moral exertion or possession capable of overcoming the inertia caused by uncertainty was disciplined emotion. Rationality unassisted by positive emotion, he was convinced, lacked the strength of conviction required to counteract doubt or other comparably powerful negative feelings such as fear.[93] "There is a disposition to undervalue emotions," Mahan wrote,

> because of their frequent transiency and lack of sequence. In so far, reproach is just; and this tendency will be particularly strong among practical peoples, whose eyes are fixed upon results, upon things accomplished. To regard emotion solely thus, however, is to depreciate power; for emotion is power. But like all power it needs to be managed, economized, guided, and disciplined. It must not be allowed to run to waste, or to be misdirected. Emotions must be brought to book, made to give an account of themselves, as shown in their fruit. They need also—and this is often overlooked—to be acquired.[94]

For Mahan, Christian virtue was not simply a matter of following rules; it was about spiritual development that was propelled by a combination of an individual's intellectual and emotional activity. Salvation was thus to be generated from internal growth, not imposed by compliance with external law. For this reason, Mahan viewed biblical scripture as no more than the counterpart to strategic principles, which is to say that they were a starting point for learning from experience, and not a strict guide to behavior. "The thought of the Way," wrote Mahan, "is one that admits and requires a large elaboration—working out—in details and in application; but it may be questioned whether one man can do this well for another. Suggestions doubtless are useful and can be made; and it is suggestion chiefly, rather than a formal plan of life, that religious reading, even of the Bible, gives to each. The most elaborate system of 'direction' can scarcely effect more than outlines, with the attendant evil of sapping individual power to comprehend personal life, and to order personal conduct."[95]

---

[93] This was implied in Mahan's biography of Nelson. His explicit statement in *The Harvest Within* may be attributable to his temporary loss of faith following a serious medical operation in 1907. See Seager, *ATM*, 574–5.
[94] Mahan, *Harvest Within*, 253.
[95] Ibid., 244.

Mahan believed that the best preceptor of true Christian consciousness, like that of effective naval command, was experience. To know Christian truth "with that conviction which alone is worthy of the name knowledge," Mahan declared, "is the result of personal experience."[96] Experience, Mahan observed, "implies expertness,—an expert. That is, the result can be reached only after patient continued testing, analogous to the experiments of Science in method, but not in fundamental spirit. For Science demands Sight, whereas Christian conviction interprets experience by Faith."[97] Experience was necessary because the full fruits of experience could not be transmitted by words. "Personal inward experiences," Mahan noted, were "seldom—almost never—fit subject for communication to others, but even the practical results of such experience, realized in thought and conclusions, may have little value outside the individual, however decisive their influence upon himself. Self-deception in such a matter is easy; the sense of proportion is readily lost; one may think too highly of his thoughts as well as of himself."[98] For these reasons, Mahan warned elsewhere that "nothing is more unpracticable than generalities."[99]

That being said, however, Mahan nonetheless maintained that "fixed and certain practical conclusions" that were the "combined outcome of experience and reflection" could "command allegiance and influence conduct" and thus "have value to fellow-combatants in the battle of life."[100] In other words, Mahan believed that an account of experience, or what in the context of his naval writing he called "history," while not equal to experience itself, could improve the capacity of individuals to learn from their own experience. We "all know well," he declared, "that, while nothing teaches like personal experience, while nothing can take its place, nevertheless the experience of each generation becomes a fresh starting point for the one which succeeds. Each new generation enters upon the heritage of its predecessor's experience; and while the transmitted experience,—the hearing of the ear,—can never equal the personal experience,—the seeing of the eye,—nevertheless the starting point of the new age is, or should be, an advance upon that of the preceding."[101]

---

[96] Ibid., 272.
[97] Ibid., 108.
[98] Ibid., v.
[99] A. T. Mahan, "The Practical in Christianity: An Address Delivered in the Church of the Holy Trinity, Middletown, Conn., Wednesday, March 22, 1899," in Mahan, *Harvest Within*, 269.
[100] Mahan, *Harvest Within*, v.
[101] Mahan, "The Practical in Christianity," 273–4.

CHAPTER FIVE

National, Transnational, and International Politics

Three men testified about the tortoise, so that makes it a turtle.

—Toyo Eicho Zenji, *Zenrin Kushu* (A Zen phrase anthology)

Once we assume that the unit of analysis is . . . a "world-system" and not the "state" or the "nation" or the "people," then much changes in the outcome of the analysis. Most specifically we shift from a concern with the attributive characteristics of states to concern with the relational characteristics of states.

—Immanuel Wallerstein, *The Modern World-System*

CHANGES OF OPINION

In examining his own time in the lesser works, Mahan came to conclusions about political-economic and governmental argument that reversed positions he had taken earlier. In 1911, Mahan conceded that he had been wrong to argue that commercial development was the prerequisite to the growth of a strong navy, which he had insisted was the case in *The Influence of Sea Power upon History*.[1] "There is one further conclusion to be drawn from the war between Japan and Russia," he wrote,

---

[1] Alfred Thayer Mahan, *The Influence of Sea Power upon History, 1660–1783* (Boston: Little, Brown, 1890), 26, 49, 82.

which contradicts a previous general impression that I myself have shared, and possibly in some degree have contributed to diffuse. That impression is, that navies depend upon maritime commerce as the cause and justification of their existence. To a certain extent, of course, this is true; and, just because true to a certain extent, the conclusion is more misleading. Because partly true, it is accepted as unqualifiedly true. Russia has little maritime commerce, at least in her own bottoms; her merchant flag is rarely seen; she has a very defective sea coast; can in no sense be called a maritime nation. Yet the Russian navy had the decisive part to play in the late war. . . . I am not particularly interested here to define the relations of commerce to a navy. It seems reasonable to say that, where merchant shipping exists, it tends logically to develop the form of protection which is called naval; but it has become perfectly evident, by concrete examples, that a navy may be necessary where there is no shipping. . . . More and more it becomes clear, that the function of navies is distinctly military and international, whatever their historical origin in particular cases.[2]

Mahan also came to conclusions in one of his lesser works that amounted to the nullification of the governmental argument that he had presented in the first volume of the "Influence of Sea Power" series, although in this case a change of mind was not admitted. In *The Influence of Sea Power upon History*, Mahan, emphasizing the historical experience of France, maintained that state action with regard to the development of sea power was crucial. In *The Influence of Sea Power upon the French Revolution and Empire* and in his biography of Nelson, his focus on the Royal Navy's success seems to have led Mahan to believe that even the most well-endowed continental power was incapable of concentrating the resources required to build and support a navy strong enough to overcome an insular power, because of the distraction of having to field an army capable of defending exposed land frontiers. Mahan stated the new position explicitly in 1902 when he wrote that "history has conclusively demonstrated the inability of a state with even a single continental frontier to compete in naval development with one that is insular, although of smaller population and resources."[3]

---

[2] A. T. Mahan, *Naval Strategy* (Boston: Little, Brown, 1911), 445–6.
[3] A. T. Mahan, "Considerations Governing the Disposition of Navies," *National Review* (July 1902), reprinted in A. T. Mahan, *Retrospect and Prospect: Studies in International Relations Naval and Political* (London: Sampson Low, Marston, 1902), 169.

Mahan's transfer of emphasis from France to Britain also made it necessary for him to change his geopolitical conception of the United States in order to characterize his own country in a manner that facilitated convincing analogy with the more successful model. In his first study of sea power, he had argued that America and France both possessed highly productive land-based economies, which distracted attention from the benefits to be gained from maritime commercial activity,[4] and that America's essential geographical character would differ from that of Britain until her two ocean seaboards were connected by a Central American canal.[5] Mahan, in short, initially thought of the United States as being a continental rather than an insular nation. Only a few months after the publication of *The Influence of Sea Power upon the French Revolution and Empire*, however, and long before the linking of the Atlantic and Pacific oceans at Panama, Mahan began to argue that America was an island power and as such was advised to look to the history of Britain for instruction.[6]

ANGLO-AMERICAN NAVAL CONSORTIUM

Mahan's presentation of Britain as an example was intended to be general rather than particular, which is to say that he believed Britain's experience during the age of sail demonstrated that sea power employed effectively paid large dividends, and not that world naval supremacy exercised by a single state should be a goal for the United States in the age of steam. This was the case for two reasons. In the first place, Mahan rejected the notion that America should build a navy comparable in size

---

[4] Mahan, *Influence of Sea Power upon History*, 38.

[5] Ibid., 33–5.

[6] A. T. Mahan, "The Isthmus and Sea Power," *Atlantic Monthly* (September 1893), reprinted in Captain A. T. Mahan, *The Interest of America in Sea Power, Present and Future* (Boston: Little, Brown, 1897), 104. For an earlier admonition to Americans to look to the example of British history, see A. T. Mahan, "The Practical Character of the United States Naval War College," address, September 1892, reprinted in Captain A. T. Mahan, *Naval Administration and Warfare: Some General Principles with Other Essays* (Boston: Little, Brown, 1908), 229. For Mahan's suggestion that in the case of the United States, insularity was a characteristic that could be acquired, see his "The Future in Relation to American Naval Power," *Harper's New Monthly Magazine* (October 1895), in Mahan, *Interest of America in Sea Power*, 143; and "The Persian Gulf and International Relations," *National Review* (September 1902), in Mahan, *Retrospect and Prospect*, 247. For Mahan's concession as late as 1900, however, that the United States still retained the characteristics of a continental power, see his "The Effect of Asiatic Conditions upon World Policies," *North American Review* (November 1900), reprinted in A. T. Mahan, *The Problem of Asia and Its Effect upon International Policies*, (Boston: Little, Brown, 1900), 197.

to that of Britain. And second, Mahan believed that the changed political and economic conditions of the late nineteenth and early twentieth centuries, compared with those of the eighteenth and early nineteenth centuries, meant that the command of the seas could be produced only through the cooperative naval action of two or more powers. Consideration of these and related questions herein include references to *The Influence of Sea Power upon History* as well as the lesser works.

Mahan's objections to the building of a navy equal to or greater in size than that of Britain were explained in an article published in December 1890. First, Mahan observed that in spite of the great wealth of the United States in absolute terms, it was "poor in proportion to its length of seaboard and its exposed points."[7] A navy large enough to secure American maritime interests on its own, in other words, could not be afforded. Second, in any case, neither Britain nor France, then the world's two leading naval powers, could deploy their full strength in the Western hemisphere "without weakening their European position or unduly exposing their colonies and commerce," a strategic fact that Mahan argued should be the "starting-point from which to calculate the strength of our own navy."[8] And finally, while he believed that a "formal alliance" between Britain and America was "out of the question," he was sure that "a cordial understanding" between the two countries would produce "co-operation beneficial to both."[9]

Mahan's positive justification for a less-than-supreme but still substantial navy had three aspects. The first was that America's geographical isolation, while not conferring absolute security by itself, when supported by a measure of force could be transformed into a considerable asset. "An estimate of what is an adequate naval force for our country," Mahan wrote in 1893, "may properly take into account the happy interval which separates both our present territory and our future aspirations from the centre of interest really vital to European states."[10] Second, while a medium-sized fleet might not be capable of providing complete security for American maritime interests, it could offer a

---

[7] A. T. Mahan, "The United States Looking Outward," *Atlantic Monthly* (December 1890), in Mahan, *Interest of America in Sea Power*, 14.
[8] Ibid., 16.
[9] Ibid., 27. See also Mahan to Leopold J. Maxse, 22 December 1902, in *The Letters and Papers of Alfred Thayer Mahan*, ed. Robert Seager II and Doris Maguire, 3 vols. (Annapolis, Md.: Naval Institute Press, 1975), iii: 50 (hereinafter cited as *LPATM*).
[10] A. T. Mahan, "Hawaii and Our Future Sea Power," *Forum* (March 1893), reprinted in Mahan, *Interest of America in Sea Power*, 54–5. See also Mahan, "The Effect of Asiatic Conditions," 182.

sufficient threat to a potential enemy to deter aggression. "Effective defense," Mahan argued in 1898, "does not consist primarily in power to protect, but in power to injure."[11] Third, the possession of a significant navy would make the United States more attractive as an ally. "Great Britain," he warned in 1894, "could not be expected reasonably to depend upon our fulfillment of the terms of an alliance . . . so long as the United States is unwilling herself to assure the security of the positions involved by the creation of an adequate force."[12]

Mahan's favoring of cooperation between Britain and the United States was based upon his conviction that no single power in the industrial era was capable of exercising naval supremacy on its own. "The circumstances of naval war," he maintained in *The Influence of Sea Power upon History*, "have changed so much within the last hundred years, that it may be doubted whether such disastrous effects on the one hand, or such brilliant prosperity on the other, as were seen in the wars between England and France, could now recur."[13] In 1894, Mahan observed that it was "improbable that control [over the seas] ever again will be exercised, as once it was, by a single nation."[14] In 1907, he noted it was "not likely, indeed, that we shall again see so predominant a naval power as Great Britain" during the Napoleonic Wars.[15] Mahan's reasons for ruling out the possibility of one nation building and maintaining a supreme navy in the twentieth century need to be examined at length.

In *The Influence of Sea Power upon History*, Mahan observed that Britain's naval successes in the eighteenth century had been attributable to the actions of a landed aristocracy, which had seen to the building and maintenance of the strongest navy that her economy and financial system could support.[16] He then noted that subsequent social and political changes in Britain had weakened the financial foundations of her naval power. "Since 1815, and especially in our own day," he wrote,

---

[11] A. T. Mahan, "Current Fallacies upon Naval Subjects," *Harper's Monthly Magazine* (June 1898), reprinted in Alfred T. Mahan, *Lessons of the War with Spain and Other Articles* (Boston: Little, Brown, 1899), 302 (see also 305); Mahan, "The Effect of Asiatic Conditions," 182–3, 189; and Mahan, *Naval Strategy*, 250.

[12] A. T. Mahan, "Possibilities of an Anglo-American Reunion," *North American Review* (November 1894), reprinted in Mahan, *Interest of America in Sea Power*, 113. See also Mahan, "The Effect of Asiatic Conditions," 180, 189, 197–8.

[13] Mahan, *Influence of Sea Power upon History*, 84.

[14] Mahan, "Possibilities of an Anglo-American Reunion," 125.

[15] Captain A. T. Mahan, *Some Neglected Aspects of War* (Boston: Little, Brown, 1907), 168. But for the incomplete naval dominance of Britain even at the height of her power in the eighteenth and early nineteenth centuries, see Mahan, *Naval Strategy*, 256, 260–1.

[16] Mahan, *Influence of Sea Power upon History*, 66.

the government of England has passed very much more into the hands of the people at large. Whether her sea power will suffer therefrom remains to be seen. Its broad basis still remains in a great trade, large mechanical industries, and an extensive colonial system. Whether a democratic government will have the foresight, the keen sensitiveness to national position and credit, the willingness to insure its prosperity by adequate outpouring of money in times of peace, all which are necessary for military preparation, is yet an open question. Popular governments are not generally favorable to military expenditure, however necessary, and there are signs that England tends to drop behind.[17]

In 1899, Mahan again took note of the unwillingness of the British electorate to provide enough money for the navy.[18] In 1902, he broadened his criticism to include the condition of the wellsprings of British power when he opined that "there is certainly an impression in America, which I share, that Great Britain for various reasons has been tending to lose ground in economical and commercial matters."[19] As early as in 1894, Mahan had concluded that "Great Britain's sea power, though still superior, has declined relatively to that of other states, and is no longer supreme."[20] In 1910, in response to the decisions that Britain's Liberal administration had made the year before to extend social welfare programs and to pay for them through radical methods of taxation, Mahan argued that "the British navy is declining, relatively, owing to the debility of a government which in the way of expenditure has assumed obligations in seeming excess of its power to meet by sound financial methods."[21]

---

[17] Ibid., 67.

[18] Mahan, *Lessons of the War with Spain*, 20.

[19] Mahan, "The Persian Gulf and International Relations," 245.

[20] Mahan, "Possibilities of an Anglo-American Reunion," 130.

[21] A. T. Mahan, *The Interest of America in International Conditions* (Boston: Little, Brown, 1910), 150. See also A. T. Mahan, *Armaments and Arbitration, or the Place of Force in the International Relations of States* (New York: Harper, 1912), 20; and Mahan to William H. Henderson, 26 December 1910, *LPATM*, iii: 371. Mahan's considerable understanding of national finance appears to have come from his father-in-law, Manlius Evans, who was a businessman and student of political economy. See Mahan to Samuel A. Ashe, 5 and 7 March 1878, *LPATM*, i: 467. For Mahan's concern with national financial affairs, see Mahan to Samuel A. Ashe, 26 November 1879, *LPATM*, i: 477. For his continued interest in national finance in general and fear of socialism in particular, see Mahan to Samuel A. Ashe, 3 January 1897, *LPATM*, ii: 483. For his dislike of the British Liberal Party, see Mahan to James R. Thursfield, 22 January 1906, *LPATM*, iii: 153–5.

Mahan placed the blame for what was perceived to be growing British weakness with respect to Germany upon the difference between their political structures, that is, on the disadvantages—from the military and naval point of view—of representative as opposed to authoritarian monarchical government. "Though vastly the richer nation," he observed in 1910, "the people of Great Britain, for the very reason of greater wealth long enjoyed, are not habituated to the economical endurance of the German; nor can the habits of individual liberty in England or America accept, unless under duress, the heavy yoke of organization, of regulation of individual action, which constitutes the power of Germany among modern states."[22]

Mahan's statement of the argument in a general form that made it relevant to American circumstances expressed long-held views and was often repeated in later years. In 1897, Mahan had maintained that representative governments, such as those existing in Britain and the United States, lacked the capacity to make adequate financial provision for "a complete scheme of national military policy, whether for offense or defense,"[23] and that the "instincts" of an insular state, with its "extensive commercial relations," were "naturally for peace, because it has so much at stake outside its shores."[24] "To prepare for war in time of peace," he maintained in 1911, "is impracticable to commercial representative nations, because the people in general will not give sufficient heed to military necessities, or to international problems, to feel the pressure which induces readiness."[25]

Commentary of this kind was bound to raise troubling questions about Mahan's views on the viability of representative government,[26] against which he provided an answer in 1912:

> I guard myself, of course, from expressing any serious dissent
> from the method of the United States and of Great Britain, in

[22] Mahan, *Interest of America in International Conditions*, 163. See also 75–6. For Mahan on the authoritarian characteristics of German political culture, see also Mahan to James R. Thursfield, 25 January 1898, *LPATM*, ii: 536–7.

[23] A. T. Mahan, "Preparedness for Naval War," *Harper's New Monthly Magazine* (September 1897), reprinted in Mahan, *Interest of America in Sea Power*, 175.

[24] Ibid., 211.

[25] Mahan, *Naval Strategy*, 447. For the danger posed by such behavior, see A. T. Mahan, *The Major Operations of the Navies in the War of American Independence* (Boston: Little Brown, 1913), 29.

[26] For more on this, see Peter Karsten, *The Naval Aristocracy: The Golden Age of Annapolis and the Emergence of Modern American Navalism* (New York: Free Press, 1972), 208–9.

annual appropriations controlled by the legislature of each successive year. It is in accord with the genius of their institutions, and therefore best suited to their practice; while it possesses the incontestable merit of preserving the guardianship of the purse which is the foundation of their edifice of liberty. In short, it is consistent with their whole scheme of government; while the drawback, that expenditures are viewed not with a single eye to national needs but with a double regard to that and to the next election, is equally characteristic and perhaps equally essential to government by the people.[27]

Mahan still held to his view that authoritarian rule was, at least in the near term, more efficient militarily than democracy. But he found safe ground in the argument that its shortcomings over time outweighed its immediate advantages. "In the long run, however," he observed in 1912,

for purposes of deliberation one man is never equal to several men. We note easily the force of a one-man power; but when he is great and distinguished, in the blaze of his efficiency we realize less easily, though we perfectly well know, the ultimate weakness of unconditioned authority. A dictator may be well enough for six months; for perpetuity and ordinary occasions let us have equals. My old instructor in navigation used to say that the average of a dozen observations is safer than to trust one you think particularly excellent. This is the theory of popular and of representative government in a nutshell. The average judgment of all the people is in the long run better than the judgment of the one wisest.[28]

Such a paean to the virtues of democracy over time, however, did not solve the problem of providing for an effective defense in the short run against the offensive action of a powerful and expansionist authoritarian state. This kind of country, when in possession of "preponderant concentrated force," Mahan wrote in 1910, "not only has its way, but it takes its way, because, whatever progress the world has made, the stage has not been reached when men or states willingly subordinate their own interests to even a reasonable regard for that of others."[29] Mahan

---

[27] Mahan, *Armaments and Arbitration,* 59–60.
[28] Ibid., 74–5.
[29] Mahan, *Interest of America in International Conditions,* 40–1.

had two responses to this dilemma. The first was a recommendation that for countries such as the United States and Britain, the appropriate policy in the event of war was to hold, mobilize, and counterattack—or in other words, a defensive grand strategy of protracted war like that of Britain during the conflict with Napoleon. "If time be, as is everywhere admitted, a supreme factor in war," he argued in *The Influence of Sea Power upon History*,

> it behooves countries whose genius is essentially not military, whose people, like all free people, object to pay for large military establishments, to see to it that they are at least strong enough to gain the time necessary to turn the spirit and capacity of their subjects into the new activities which war calls for. If the existing force by land or sea is strong enough so to hold out, even though at a disadvantage, the country may rely upon its natural resources and strength coming into play for whatever they are worth,—its numbers, its wealth, its capacities of every kind.[30]

Mahan's second answer to the question posed by the inadequacy of fiscal support for the adequate defense of vital interests was transnational cooperation. "Each man and each state," he observed, "is independent just so far as there is strength to go alone, and no farther. When this limit is reached, if farther steps must be made, co-operation must be accepted."[31] Such a course was favored in the case of the United States and Britain by the accord that existed between the two countries, which Mahan believed was based in large part upon political and cultural affinity. In 1890, he explained that "a cordial recognition of the similarity of character and ideas will give birth to sympathy, which in turn will facilitate a co-operation."[32] In 1894, Mahan identified an "unmistakable growth of mutual kindly feelings between Great Britain and the United States."[33] In 1897, he maintained that a deep sympathy existed between Britain and the United States that was "founded upon common fundamental ideas of law and justice."[34] In 1900, Mahan declared that "both the signs of the times and obvious

---

[30] Mahan, *Influence of Sea Power upon History*, 48.
[31] Mahan, "The Effect of Asiatic Conditions," 177–8.
[32] Mahan, "The United States Looking Outward," 27.
[33] Mahan, "Possibilities of an Anglo-American Reunion," 108.
[34] Mahan, "Preparedness for Naval War," 185.

motives for action point to a probably permanent co-operation between the communities which speak the English tongue."[35] And in 1910, he noted that "common political traditions," as well as "common interest" were the main props of British and American "mutual support."[36]

Besides political and cultural affinity, Mahan held that Anglo-American friendship was encouraged by the absence of major conflicting interests and the existence of strong common ones. The financial weakness of the British state, he argued, meant that it lacked the money to pursue an active policy of overseas territorial expansion. Britain, Mahan observed in 1910, was, among other things, "replete to satiety with colonial possessions" and thus had "no adequate stimulus to aggression, least of all against the United States."[37] But in addition, there was the attraction of the ability of combined action to produce a preponderance of force sufficient to achieve the benefits of naval supremacy realized by Britain alone a century before. "To Great Britain and the United States," he wrote in 1894, ". . . is intrusted a maritime interest . . . which demands, as one of the conditions of its exercise and its safety, the organized force adequate to control the general course of events at sea."[38]

Mahan rejected the notion of a conventional treaty agreement, however. "Relations between Great Britain and ourselves, that rested upon mutual understanding of common interests and common traditions," he wrote in 1900, "would far exceed in potential force any formal alliance,—which for many reasons would be greatly to be deprecated."[39] Anglo-American cooperation, Mahan further argued, though "not formal," would nevertheless be "clearly conscious."[40] "As the world is now

---

[35] A. T. Mahan, "The Problem of Asia" (III), *Harper's New Monthly Magazine* (May 1900), reprinted in Mahan, *Problem of Asia*, 145. See also Mahan, "The Effect of Asiatic Conditions," 186–8, 195–8.

[36] Mahan, *Interest of America in International Conditions*, 80. Mahan had been an advocate of Anglo-American cooperation for some years. See, for example, Mahan to Samuel A. Ashe, 11 March 1885, *LPATM*, i: 593. For Mahan's belief that "substantial identity of aims" was necessary to promote "cordial esteem," see Mahan to James Ford Rhodes, 26 April 1897, *LPATM*, ii: 503.

[37] Mahan, *Interest of America in International Conditions*, 75–6. See also Mahan to Charles W. Stewart, 19 March 1909, *LPATM*, iii: 291.

[38] Mahan, "Possibilities of an Anglo-American Reunion," 111. See also Mahan, "The Effect of Asiatic Conditions," 197, and Mahan to Theodore Roosevelt, 27 December 1904 and 20 July 1906, *LPATM*, iii: 113, 165.

[39] Mahan, "The Effect of Asiatic Conditions," 195–6. For Mahan's opposition to American involvement in formal alliances, see Mahan to Leopold J. Maxse, 28 April 1903, *LPATM*, iii: 59.

[40] Ibid., 123. See also 109, 181.

balanced," he wrote in 1902, "the British Empire is in external matters our natural though not our formal ally."[41] For Mahan, in other words, the condition of mutual interests and support defined what could be called an Anglo-American naval consortium. Within this relationship, the status of the U.S. Navy was clearly to be that of junior partner. America, Mahan wrote in 1912, could "properly cede superiority, because to the British Islands naval power is vital in a sense in which it is not to the United States."[42]

Mahan's definition of American naval security in terms of an Anglo-American naval consortium rather than a supreme American navy meant that he viewed the rising power of the German navy in terms of its effect on the British and American naval relationship, not only with respect to separate British or American strategic concerns. In 1909, the Liberal government's introduction of a comprehensive and consequently expensive program of social reform, which threatened adequate spending on the navy, prompted him to contemplate the possibility that Britain, in the face of a Germany that was very strong at sea, might step aside on any but the most direct challenge to her vital concerns. In 1911, Mahan thus wrote that "if social and political conditions in Great Britain develop as they now promise, the British navy will probably decline in relative strength, so that it will not venture to withstand the German on any broad lines of policy, but only in the narrowest sense of immediate British interests. Even this condition may disappear, for it seems as if the national life of Great Britain were waning at the same time that of Germany is waxing."[43]

In 1912, Mahan speculated that the decisive defeat of Britain by Germany, or vice versa, would produce a situation in which the victorious power would be able to defend its own vital maritime interests at home while at the same time having the capacity to project significant force into the Western Hemisphere. Although not stated as such, it is clear from his other writing that Mahan's concern was addressed to the

---

[41] A. T. Mahan, "Retrospect and Prospect," *The World's Work* (February 1902), reprinted in Mahan, *Retrospect and Prospect*, 34. See also Mahan to Horatio G. Dohrman, 15 July 1912, *LPATM*, iii: 468. For Mahan's view that America might have to back Britain against Germany in her own interest, see Mahan to John P. Merrell, 23 July 1909, *LPATM*, iii: 307–8.

[42] Mahan, *Armaments and Arbitration*, 180. See also 194; Mahan to William H. Henderson, 1 June 1902, *LPATM*, iii: 27–8; and Mahan, *Naval Strategy*, 54, 331–2.

[43] Mahan, *Naval Strategy*, 110.

threat of Germany.[44] In any case, he noted that the destruction of the European naval balance would leave the upholding of the Monroe Doctrine, which he regarded as the sheet anchor of America's foreign policy, solely to "the United States battle fleet."[45] In the face of this new condition, America would then require a "two-ocean" navy to defend vital interests in the Atlantic and Caribbean and—given the demonstration of Japanese naval power in the Russo-Japanese War—in the Pacific.[46] At this same time, Mahan was distressed by reductions in the pace of American battleship construction that were the result of the congressional elections of 1910, which placed the anti–big-ship Democratic Party in control of the House of Representatives.[47] He was also troubled by Japanese immigration to the West Coast because he believed it would lead to an Asian majority population and a clash with Japan over the ownership of continental American territory.[48]

Particular uneasiness about the possibility of Britain's elimination as a major naval power, concerns about the course of domestic politics, and fears about Japan prompted Mahan in late 1912 to call for America to maintain a "preponderant navy."[49] The purposes of such a force, however, were regional and defensive: the protection of American interests in the Caribbean and preservation of American sovereignty on the Pacific coast of the continental United States. Insofar as the latter

---

[44] Mahan to Carter FitzHugh, 7 June 1911, *LPATM*, iii: 410; Mahan to Theodore Roosevelt, 19 June 1911, *LPATM*, iii: 412; Mahan to Henry Cabot Lodge, 8 January 1912, *LPATM*, iii: 443–4; and Mahan to John Bassett Moore, 26 February 1912, *LPATM*, iii: 444–5. For Mahan's view, on the other hand, that Germany did not pose an immediate threat to the United States even though it was a significant potential threat, see Mahan to Bouverie F. Clark, 23 July 1909 and 10 March 1910, *LPATM*, iii: 307–8, 334; and Mahan to the editor of the *Daily Mail*, c. June 1910, *LPATM*, iii: 345.

[45] Mahan, *Naval Strategy*, 363.

[46] For Mahan's flirtation with this issue, see Mahan, *Naval Strategy*, 43, 54. For Mahan's view of America's naval strategic situation in the Pacific and its relation to that of the Atlantic and Caribbean, see Mahan to Henry C. Taylor, 7 December 1903, *LPATM*, iii: 80. For Mahan's partisan motives for justifying the construction of a larger battle fleet in terms of two-ocean requirements, see Mahan to the editor of the *New York Times*, 2 April and 22 May 1912, *LPATM*, iii: 453–4, 457–9; and Mahan to Samuel A. Ashe, 7 June 1912, *LPATM*, iii: 465. For Mahan's fears about Japan, see Mahan to Stephen B. Luce, 17 June 1908, *LPATM*, iii: 251.

[47] Mahan to Samuel A. Ashe, 7 June 1912, *LPATM*, iii: 465; Mahan to Horatio G. Dohrman, 15 July 1912, *LPATM*, iii: 468–9; and Harold Sprout and Margaret Sprout, *The Rise of American Naval Power, 1776–1918* (Princeton: Princeton University Press, 1966), 290–5.

[48] Robert Seager II, *Alfred Thayer Mahan: The Man and His Letters* (Annapolis, Md.: Naval Institute Press, 1977), 478–80, 488.

[49] Mahan, *Major Operations of the Navies*, 4.

issue was concerned, Mahan justified reliance on a navy that was superior to that of Japan on the grounds that such a course would be cheaper
and more effective than the deployment of an army.[50] Moreover, he
concluded this discussion with the observation that American security
was thus to be "staked upon naval adequacy."[51] Mahan's notion of
American naval preponderance was thus by no means intended as a
challenge to continued British worldwide naval supremacy.[52]

UNCERTAIN PROPHET

When it came to the subject of the future course of international relations, Mahan presented several alternatives that were based upon incompatible assumptions. In the first place, he conceived of an international economy based upon overseas trade, in which the commercial
interests of countries were both opposed through competition and in-
tertwined because of mutual benefit. "The unmolested course of commerce, reacting upon itself," Mahan observed in 1902, "has contributed
also to its own rapid development, a result furthered by the prevalence
of a purely economical conception of national greatness during the
larger part of the century. This, with the vast increase in rapidity of
communication, has multiplied and strengthened the bonds knitting
the interests of nations to one another, till the whole now forms an
articulated system, not only of prodigious size and activity, but of an
excessive sensitiveness, unequaled in former ages."[53]

For Mahan, the combination of economic interdependence and his
belief that the populations of industrial countries lacked the moral stam-
ina to endure the hardships that would ensue in the event of protracted
war prompted him to argue against the notion that economic imperatives worked only in favor of great-power conflict. "National nerves are
exasperated by the delicacy of financial situations," he wrote in 1902,
"and national resistance to hardship is sapped by generations that have
known war only by the battlefield, not in the prolonged endurance of

---

[50] Ibid., 5.
[51] Ibid., 5.
[52] In any case, Mahan held that "preponderance" was less than "paramountcy." See A. T.
Mahan, "The Monroe Doctrine: A Consistent Development," *National Review* (February
1902), reprinted in Mahan, *Naval Administration and Warfare*, 396–7. For Mahan's criticism in 1910 of calls for an American policy of "supremacy in the Pacific," see Mahan, *Interest of America in International Conditions*, 192.
[53] Mahan, "Considerations Governing the Disposition of Navies," 143–4.

privation and straitness extending through years and reaching every class of the community. The preservation of commercial and financial interests constitutes now a political consideration of the first importance, making for peace and deterring from war."[54] "War has ceased to be the natural, or even normal, condition of nations," Mahan concluded, "and military considerations are simply accessory and subordinate to the other greater interests, economical and commercial, which they assure and so subserve."[55] A month later, he declared that "as for economical rivalry, let it be confined to its own methods, eschewing force."[56]

A decade afterwards, however, Mahan argued that competition between Western great powers for control over Asian and African territories that were coveted for their potential economic value, over the long run, might provide the grounds for a major conflict. "It is the great amount of unexploited raw material in territories politically backward, and now imperfectly possessed by the nominal owners," he observed in 1912, "which at the present moment constitutes the temptation and the impulse to war of European states."[57] Mahan also feared that the governments of his day were all susceptible to public opinion, which when excited could prompt a decision for war even when materially disadvantageous. "I hold that the interest of the nation is indeed the business of the government," he insisted, "but that the danger of war proceeds mainly from the temper of the people, which, when roused, disregards self-interest."[58] "In short," Mahan went on to say, "the inciting causes of war in our day are moral."[59]

Mahan rejected the idea that conflict could be avoided through international law and arbitration.[60] This left him with no other means of

[54] Ibid., 144. See also A. T. Mahan, "The Hague Conference of 1907, and the Question of Immunity for Belligerent Merchant Shipping," *National Review* (July 1907), reprinted in Mahan, *Some Neglected Aspects of War,* 173, 179; and Mahan to editor of the *New York Times,* c. 2 November 1910, *LPATM,* iii: 366.
[55] Mahan, "The Persian Gulf and International Relations," 249. See also 248; and Mahan, "The Hague Conference of 1907," 181.
[56] Mahan, "The Persian Gulf and International Relations," 249. But for the later weakening of Mahan's commitment to free trade, see Mahan to Bouverie F. Clark, 11 September 1908, *LPATM,* iii: 263.
[57] Mahan, *Armaments and Arbitration,* 110–11. See also A. T. Mahan, "Motives to Imperial Federation," *National Review and the International Monthly* (May 1902), reprinted in Mahan, *Retrospect and Prospect,* 111.
[58] Mahan, *Armaments and Arbitration,* 124.
[59] Ibid., 126.
[60] Ibid., Preface and passim. See also A. T. Mahan, "The Peace Conference and the Moral Aspect of War," *North American Review* (October 1899), reprinted in Mahan, *Lessons of the War with Spain;* and A. T. Mahan, *Some Neglected Aspects of War.*

settling disputes except force wielded by sovereign powers acting in the pursuit of their individual concerns. At the same time, Mahan posited the existence of an international economic system that conferred large if differential benefits upon all of its constituents. Both particular and general interests were thus served by any naval coalition strong enough to deter aggression, impose international order to facilitate the political and economic development of backward regions in peacetime, and provide security to the bulk of the world's overseas trading activity in the event of hostilities. Mahan's Anglo-American naval consortium was, within this frame of reference, no more than a transnational means to achieve an even greater transnational end, which was described when he declared in 1912 that "force must be used for the benefit of the community, of the commonwealth of the world."[61]

Mahan's worldview, however, had another, less optimistic side. In opposition to his vision of an international order was his premonition—albeit reserved and fluctuating in strength—of a future cataclysmic collision between Western and Eastern civilizations. "Our Pacific slope, and the Pacific colonies of Great Britain," he warned as early as in 1894,

> with an instinctive shudder have felt the threat, which able Europeans have seen in the teeming multitudes of central and northern Asia; while their overflow into the Pacific Islands shows that not only westward by land, but also eastward by sea, the flood may sweep. I am not careful, however, to search into the details of a great movement, which indeed may never come, but whose possibility, in existing conditions, looms large upon the horizon of the future, and against which the only barrier will be the warlike spirit of the representatives of civilization.[62]

In 1897, Mahan contemplated the rise of Asian states that were equipped with Western weapons, methods of war, and political organization, and the potentially dangerous implications for the West of these developments.[63] But in 1900, Mahan considered the possibility that

---

[61] Mahan, *Armaments and Arbitration*, 117. See also Mahan, "Possibilities of an Anglo-American Reunion," 112–13, Mahan, "The Problem of Asia" (I, II), and Mahan, "The Effect of Asiatic Conditions," 26, 77, 90–1, 163.

[62] Mahan, "Possibilities of an Anglo-American Reunion," 123–4. For the French failure to settle their North American holdings as the reason for British victory in the colonial wars of the eighteenth century, which may have been the historical source of Mahan's anxieties about Asian immigration, see Mahan, *Influence of Sea Power upon History*, 283.

[63] Mahan, "A Twentieth-Century Outlook," *Harper's New Monthly Magazine* (September 1897) reprinted in Mahan, *The Interest of America in Sea Power*, 234–7.

conflict might be avoided through Asian assimilation of Western culture and the subsequent development of a world civilization.[64] And in 1901, he described America's role as one of mediator between Europe and Asia.[65]

Mahan treated the German question in counterpoint to his speculations about greater conflicts. He always believed that German militarism posed a general threat to peace.[66] On the other hand, prior to the exposure of Russian corruption and weakness in the Russo-Japanese War, Mahan in 1900 had called for cooperation between the Teutonic nations—Germany, Britain, and the United States—supported by Japan against what he regarded as a dangerously powerful and expansionist Russia.[67] He was also convinced that German aggressiveness had promoted competition between European countries that had the beneficial effect of strengthening Western civilization to withstand a future challenge from Asia for world supremacy. To German commercial and naval development since the foundation of the empire in 1871, Mahan argued in 1907, "we owe the military impulse which has been transmitted everywhere to the forces of sea and land," an effect for which "too great gratitude cannot be felt" because it had "braced and organized Western civilization" for the coming conflict with the East.[68]

After a decade of lying fallow, Mahan's worst fears about the Asian threat were rekindled by anxiety about the emergence of Japan as a major naval and military power and about Japanese immigration to the American West Coast.[69] "It may be that the future has in store the wreck of nationalities," he wrote in 1912, "and agglomeration of peoples in the way described; but the period of transition, like that from

---

[64] Mahan, "The Problem of Asia" (II), 90–1. See also Mahan to John S. Barnes, 21 July 1898, *LPATM*, ii: 566.

[65] A. T. Mahan, *Types of Naval Officers Drawn from the History of the British Navy; With Some Account of the Conditions of Naval Warfare at the Beginning of the Eighteenth Century, and of Its Subsequent Development during the Sail Period* (Boston: Little, Brown, 1901), ix.

[66] Mahan, "The United States Looking Outward," 8; Mahan, "Current Fallacies upon Naval Subjects," 289–98; Mahan, "The Persian Gulf and International Relations," 245–6; and Mahan, *Interest of America in International Conditions*, 40, 42–3, 81–2, 163–4, 172–3.

[67] Mahan, "The Problem of Asia" (II–III), 44, 63, 104, 108, 133; and Mahan to Leopold J. Maxse, 12 and 14 June 1902, *LPATM*, iii: 29, 32.

[68] Captain A. T. Mahan, *From Sail to Steam: Recollections of Naval Life* (New York: Harper and Brothers, 1907), 9–10. See also Mahan, "Possibilities of an Anglo-American Reunion," 122–4, 234–7; Mahan, "The Problem of Asia" (II), 73–4, 77, 90–1, 94–5; Mahan, *Armaments and Arbitration*, 8–10, 120, 142–3; and Mahan to Leopold J. Maxse, 10 May 1907, *LPATM*, iii: 211.

[69] Mahan to Theodore Roosevelt, 19 June 1911 and 2 December 1911, *LPATM*, iii: 411, 436; Mahan to Bouverie F. Clark, 12 March 1912, *LPATM*, iii: 448; and Mahan to Samuel A. Ashe, 7 June 1912, *LPATM*, iii: 465.

handicraft to factory system, will be one of disorganization which will leave Europe—and America—weakened for the collision between European and Asiatic civilizations. This not only impends, but has begun, and in it the strength of Europe is the principle of nationality, developed as it now is."[70] The expression of such views in the same volume— in the same breath, as it were—with his descriptions of a world community based upon common economic interests juxtaposed propositions that were strongly opposed, which was consistent with Mahan's view that the contemplation of contradictory lines of thought was a necessary aspect of constructive thinking about events that had yet to happen.

In general, Mahan believed in the existence of "determinative conditions" whose effect was to "shape and govern the whole range of incidents, often in themselves apparently chaotic in combination, and devoid of guidance by any adequate controlling forces." He considered the tasks of identifying those forces and comprehending their dynamics, however, to be difficult ones when dealing with the past, and even more so when contemplating the future. "In history entirely past," Mahan went on to observe in 1900, "where an issue has been reached sufficiently definite to show that one period has ended and another begun, it is possible for a careful observer to detect, and with some precision to formulate, the leading causes, and to trace the interaction which has produced the result. It is obviously much less easy to discover the character and to fix the inter-relation of the elements acting in the present; and still more to indicate the direction of their individual movement, from which conjecture may form some conception as to what shall issue as the resultant of forces. There is here all the difference between history and prophecy."[71]

The alternative to intelligent speculation, on the other hand, was ignorant or partisan exercises in prediction, and probably for this reason Mahan conceded that need for the former, for all its drawbacks, was "urgent."[72] But while he accepted the legitimacy of forecasting in spite of the doubtful character of its products, Mahan warned that rigorous

[70] Mahan, *Armaments and Arbitration*, 142–3.

[71] Mahan, "The Problem of Asia" (Preface), vi. See also A. T. Mahan, "Lessons of the War with Spain" (Introductory), *McClure's Magazine* (December 1898–April 1899), reprinted in Mahan, *Lessons of the War with Spain*, 21–2.

[72] Ibid., vii. For Mahan's increasing doubts at this time about the value of punditry, his own included, see Mahan to Theodore Roosevelt, 12 March 1901, *LPATM*, ii: 707–8.

thinking might involve the consideration of multiple sets of premises and the generation, as a consequence, of several, possibly conflicting, and even mutually exclusive, projections. "In order to [gain] efficiency of action, whether in personal or in corporate life," Mahan argued in 1900,

> we have to recognize the coincident necessities of taking long views and of confining ourselves to short ones. The two ideas, although in contradiction logically, are in practice and in effect complementary, as are the centripetal and centrifugal forces of the universe; unless both are present, something is wanting to the due balance of judgment and of decision. This is, indeed, but one of many illustrations that the philosophy of life is best expressed in paradox. It is by frank acceptance of contrary truths, embracing both without effort to blend them, that we can best direct our course, as individuals or as nations, to successful issues.[73]

"Truth—that is, a right conclusion, or solution—is most surely to be reached," Mahan later wrote in 1911, "by grasping both the ideas, which underlie the opposing statements; grasping them, I mean, in their full force, even in their extreme force and impression, such as the two expressions convey."[74]

Mahan's views of 1900 could be interpreted to cover a case in which events were being shaped simultaneously by two different dynamics working in opposing directions but at different rates, thus producing conflicting outcomes but at different times. This would explain his description in 1912 of a world in which overseas trade was promoting international peace and cooperation in the present and near future while he contemplated the increasing long-term prospects of cataclysmic conflict between East and West. Mahan's even stronger statement of 1911 was applicable to the putting forward of propositions that could be considered to be opposed diametrically in the same time. He could thus argue in one volume that competition for control over potential markets in underdeveloped areas of the world formed the main grounds

---

[73] Ibid., 1.

[74] Mahan, *Naval Strategy*, 386. "Altogether both my judgment and my sympathies," wrote Mahan about an issue of current foreign policy, "are in a somewhat chaotic state; but chaos, after all, is a boiling of materials, which may at last run out into a mould, in proper proportions." Mahan to Leopold J. Maxse, 17 June 1904, *LPATM*, iii: 99.

for war between great powers and also with equal conviction that "the inciting causes of war" were not economic but moral.[75]

With respect to the question of the political role of God, Mahan was no more certain than about the future course of world events, and thus no less contradictory. In 1897, he wondered whether or not "the ebb and flow of human affairs" was controlled by "mysterious impulses the origin of which is sought by some in personal Providence" or "by some laws not yet fully understood."[76] In 1900, he went so far as to argue that even the "least presumptuous" might view the American extension of sovereignty over the Philippines as the work of "the hand of Providence."[77] On the other hand, in 1907 Mahan maintained in unequivocal terms that he did not believe that God's will could be divined from the outcome of international events. War as "a final appeal to the judgment of God," he observed, "directly traverses my own position, which is, that, a case of possible war arising, God has given us a conscience, with revealed data, and necessary faculties for decision; I, therefore, should no more expect enlightenment as to His judgment upon the case, by recourse to War, than I should by tossing a penny."[78]

[75] Mahan, *Armaments and Arbitration*, 110–11, 116, 124, 126.
[76] Mahan, "A Twentieth-Century Outlook," 243.
[77] Mahan, "Effect of Asiatic Conditions," 175.
[78] A. T. Mahan, "War from the Christian Standpoint," paper read before the Church Congress, Providence, R.I., 15 November 1900, reprinted in Mahan, *Some Neglected Aspects of War*, 103–4.

CHAPTER SIX

The Uses of History and Theory

He has made it all so clear,
It takes a long time to catch the point.

—Mumon Ekai, *Mumonkan* (*The Gateless Gate*)

Correcter prognoses will generally issue from the judgments of those
with better knowledge of mankind.

Can one learn this knowledge? Yes; some can. Not, however, by taking a course in it, but through "*experience.*"—Can someone else be a
man's teacher in this? Certainly. From time to time he gives him the
right *tip.*—This is what "learning" and "teaching" are like here.—What
one acquires here is not a technique; one learns correct judgments.
There are also rules, but they do not form a system, and only experi-
enced people can apply them right. Unlike calculating rules.

What is most difficult here is to put this indefiniteness, correctly and
unfalsified, into words.

—Ludwig Wittgenstein, *Philosophical Investigations*

COMPLEXITY, CONTINGENCY, CHANGE, AND CONTRADICTION

Mahan transformed naval history by breaking the monopoly held by accounts of derring-do with serious analyses of naval grand strategy and the art and science of naval command. He thus invented historically based and broadly focused international security studies, which differed from earlier writing about military affairs through its relationship of policy and operations to political, political-economic, and governmental questions on a global scale. He also articulated a sophisticated approach to the problem of leadership in war, in effect applying the work of earlier writers on land warfare to conflict at sea. Mahan's role as a pioneer and extender of the work of others has been widely recognized, but the main intellectual substance of his work has been misunderstood and thus either ignored or misused. The general failure to engage his thought accurately is in large part attributable to the complexity of his exposition, the difficulties inherent in his methods of dealing with several forms of contingency, changes in his position on certain major issues, and his contradictory predictions about the future and application of strategic principles.

Complexity was mainly a matter of Mahan's analysis having several components. Mahan sometimes wrote of history teaching lessons or of the lessons of history.[1] His chief goal, however, was to address difficult questions that were not susceptible to convincing elucidation through simple reasoning by analogy. He thus viewed history less as a ready-made instructor than as a medium that had to be worked by the appropriate intellectual tools. Mahan's analytical instruments of choice were five kinds of argument: political, political-economic, governmental, strategic, and professional. The five arguments were divided into two groups that dealt with different subjects. The first three were concerned with naval grand strategy (i.e., naval power, economic development, and international relations, and their interconnectedness). The last two dealt primarily with matters related to the art and science of command. In addition to these multiple major arguments, Mahan's approach was

---

[1] A. T. Mahan, *The Influence of Sea Power upon History, 1660–1783* (Boston: Little, Brown, 1890), 2, 11, 21, 83–4, 89; A. T. Mahan, *The Influence of Sea Power upon the French Revolution and Empire, 1793–1812*, 2 vols. (Boston: Little, Brown, 1892), i: 119, 201; A. T. Mahan, *Types of Naval Officers Drawn from the History of the British Navy; With Some Account of the Conditions of Naval Warfare at the Beginning of the Eighteenth Century, and of Its Subsequent Development during the Sail Period* (Boston: Little, Brown, 1901), vii; A. T. Mahan, *Sea Power in Its Relations to the War of 1812*, 2 vols. (Boston: Little, Brown, 1905), i: v, 327; ii: 208; A. T. Mahan, *The Problem of Asia and Its Effect upon International Policies* (Boston: Little, Brown, 1900), vi; A. T. Mahan, *From Sail to Steam: Recollections of Naval Life* (New York: Harper and Brothers, 1907), 282; A. T. Mahan, "Retrospect upon the War between Japan and Russia," *National Review* (May 1906), and A. T. Mahan, "The Practical Character of the United States Naval War College," address, September 1892, reprinted in *Naval Administration and Warfare: Some General Principles with Other Essays* (Boston: Little, Brown, 1908), 167, 229; A. T. Mahan, *Naval Strategy* (Boston: Little, Brown, 1911), 115, 383; and A. T. Mahan, *The Major Operations of the Navies in the War of American Independence* (Boston: Little, Brown, 1913), v, 4.

characterized by the complexity of his handling of certain important subsidiary issues: British naval supremacy, naval supremacy in general, decisive battle, sea power, and warship design and procurement.

Attentiveness to governmental argument reveals that the "Influence of Sea Power" quartet was not unified around the theme of the rise of British naval supremacy. The principal thrust of the first volume in the series was that proper action by the French state delivered success in the American Revolution. In the second book in the series, Pitt's formulation of a grand strategy of economic attrition and protracted war enabled Britain to survive a Napoleonic onslaught that she might otherwise have lost. In the third book, Mahan focused on the necessity of having extraordinary operational leadership in order to convert naval superiority into naval supremacy. And finally, the point of the concluding work was that a relatively small investment by the American state in a larger navy would have averted disaster—which was to say that British naval supremacy could have been neutralized in the Western Hemisphere, under the prevailing circumstances of a major war in Europe that had reached the point of crisis, by a larger but still modest and therefore politically practicable U.S. Navy.

Mahan had, in the course of discussing other things, explained how Britain had attained naval supremacy and then used it to her very great advantage with decisive results in a succession of wars in the eighteenth and early nineteenth centuries. The reluctance of late-nineteenth- and early-twentieth-century popular governments to spend money on defense, however, convinced him that Britain's success in the preindustrial era could not be replicated in the industrial age by any single power. Therefore, naval supremacy, if it was to exist and play an important role in international relations, would have to be the product of cooperation between two or more states. For a variety of reasons, Mahan believed that Britain and the United States would synchronize their naval activity without the benefit of formal agreements, creating a transnational naval consortium.

Mahan's view of grand strategy, however, was not limited to the question of how to obtain and use either nationally or transnationally based naval supremacy, his references to the large benefits to be gained by "control of the sea" notwithstanding. Mahan was convinced that in war, a country with a substantial battle fleet would be capable of forcing an opponent with a superior navy to maintain its guard, which was bound to be physically arduous and fiscally onerous, as well as militarily perilous, and thus of strategic consequence. It was for this reason that he placed so much importance upon decisive battle, which was the only means by which such a dangerous situation could be ended. In peace, by the same token, even the possession of a small battle fleet under the right geographical and political circumstances, as in the case of the United States before the War of 1812, might be sufficient to deter a more powerful and even supreme naval power from risking hostilities by provocative actions. Mahan even went so far as to argue that the existence of a small but efficient American battle fleet in his own time would improve his country's value to Britain as an ally—this before the concept of using inferior naval strength as a means of gaining positive diplomatic leverage was used by German naval leaders to justify the expansion of their own navy.[2]

Other important concepts that Mahan also handled in a complex and therefore prone to be misunderstood way were "sea power" and "naval power." In his work, the terms were on occasion treated as near equivalents, and blame for the tendency to conflate the two cannot, therefore, be attributed solely to careless reading. But Mahan nonetheless considered sea power and naval power to be different phenomena. Sea power was the combination of the activities of world trade generated by an international economy and world-trade defense by a national navy or transnational naval consortium. Because this phenomenon was driven by individuals or groups in search of private gain, Mahan saw it as self-sustaining. Naval power, on the other hand, was organized force created by particular governments—that is, a subset of sea power. Given the political conditions of the day, government action was the product of deliberations between an informed leadership that understood its importance and a representative legislature that was predisposed to limit expenditure.

For Mahan, the critical factor was the attitude of the latter—the democratic propensity to spend inadequately on defense not only made it necessary to define naval supremacy in transnational terms in the twentieth century but prompted his formulation of political, political-economic, and governmental argument as a means of educating legislators and thus moderating their parsimony in naval matters. Mahan believed, however, that even the most persuasive polemics were incapable of sustaining the prolonged and consistent effort required to support a first-class navy. He thus insisted that the growth of export manufacture,

---

[2] V. R. Berghahn, *Germany and the Approach of War in 1914*, 2nd ed. (New York: St. Martin's, 1993), 52.

a merchant marine to transport it, and colonial markets were needed in order to create an economic interest that was strong enough to exert a significant influence on the electorate. In Mahan's view, here was the political connection between the economic component of sea power and naval power.

Mahan's nineteenth-century sense of fiscal probity and economic limitation—as well as a degree of technical conservatism—probably propelled much of his opposition to the growth in the dimensions and expense of warships. Repeated large increases in the size of the navy's budget, he was convinced, had the potential to price even a modest battle fleet out of the market of what Americans would consider to be viable public policy. In addition, he had long feared the deleterious effects of a navy that was concerned to an excessive degree with technological innovation, and he detested the corruption that characterized the U.S. Navy's relations with private contractors. The combination of these factors seems to have blinded him to the emergence of naval armaments manufacture as an economic and therefore political force capable of serving as a supplement to, or even in place of, that marshaled by maritime commercial interests. Mahan, in other words, for the reasons just given, failed to anticipate the implications of the development—evident in his own day—of what was to become the military-industrial complex.

Mahan's political and political-economic arguments suggested that the development of naval power was determined by large structural factors, with little or nothing left to the play of chance and circumstance—that is, contingency. Mahan's governmental argument, on the other hand, played a key role in Mahan's conception of naval grand strategy, because it offset the deterministic tendencies of political and political-economic argument by giving due weight to the role of human agency in the shaping of events. Although Mahan recognized that financial and economic conditions formed the boundaries of policy in peace and strategy in war, he was convinced that within the realm so established, decision-making by political and naval elites mattered. His view of historical process could thus be likened to a game in which the dice were loaded but not to such an extent that the outcomes were preordained absolutely—under these circumstances, determinism and contingency were complementary rather than mutually exclusive.

Mahan's approach to the art and science of command, embodied in his strategic and professional arguments, was informed by his recognition that contingency in war precluded mechanistic prescription as the basis of operational decision-making. His strategic argument was made through statements of principle and examinations of their application through extended historical narratives, which revealed both variation and exception. His naval professional argument was that operational decision-making was of critical importance to success in war and that carrying out this function was the job of naval officer-executives. The intersection of the two was to be found in the education of naval leadership, wherein strategic argument established a starting point for learning that would improve the judgment of those entrusted with making command decisions.

John Locke articulated the conventional distinction between acts of knowledge and those of judgment: an act of knowledge is based upon certain understanding, while an act of judgment occurs when knowledge is uncertain or incomplete, necessity demands action, and the shortfall in knowledge must be made good by presumption.[3] Mahan knew that in war, the difficulties posed by uncertainty or incompleteness of information were compounded by fear of dire consequences in the event of decision-making error. The faculty of judgment, therefore, had to be paired with will in order to overcome timidity that would delay or prevent action. The synthesis of judgment and will was intelligent emotion—or, in a word, intuition. When the degrees of uncertainty and danger were extremely high as they were likely to be at a time of crisis during a battle or campaign, extraordinary intuition was required to promote rapid and decisive command that transcended mere assertion of judgment to become creative performance, or in other words, an artistic act. Such intuition about matters naval was optimally the product of war experience. Mahan believed that in peacetime, the ability to improve intuition from war experience could be developed by education that was based upon the study of history.

Mahan's concern with the enhancement of the ability to learn, as opposed to the formulation of doctrine, meant that theory was an auxiliary—it served as a means rather than an end. Mahan posited the existence of immutable principles of strategy, such as "concentration of force," but these were few, platitudinous, and drawn from the works of others. As counsels of obvious virtue they defy meaningful criticism, and as derivatives they are not distinguishing properties of his thought.

---

[3] John Locke, "Book Four: Of Knowledge and Opinion," in *An Essay Concerning Human Understanding*, abridged and ed. A. D. Woozley (Cleveland, Ohio: Meridian, 1964; first published 1690), 403.

In his lesser works, which were for the most part about current events and produced to satisfy the tastes of casual readers, Mahan invoked principle to lend support to punditry and speculation. But in the "Influence of Sea Power" series and his volume of Naval War College lectures, the main subject was the distant past, the main intended audience naval decision-makers in fact or in training, and the task at hand the development of a temperament suitable for leadership in war. Here, what mattered most was not the principles as such, but their practical application.

Application could be described only through the examination of many case studies. Accounts of past experience were not used to generate principles or theories that could then stand independently in place of the originating process, but rather the reverse: principles or theories were the starting point for the study of accounts of past experience.[4] The main analytical subjects of this narrative were the difficulties posed by contingency and insufficiency of information and the rational and emotional instruments of command that were required, if not to overcome them, then to mitigate their negative effects. Mahan was concerned with the particularity of applying principles, not the generalizing that was the basis of their formulation. And the goal of coming to terms with the problem of application was not mere intellectual comprehension, but a combination of understanding and passion that produced an artistic capacity to act quickly and decisively.

Mahan changed his views on two issues of major significance. In *The Influence of Sea Power upon History*, he maintained that a grand strategy based upon a proper understanding of the significance of sea power would have enabled France to have achieved naval supremacy in spite of the best efforts of Britain. In the same work, Mahan also argued that the primary justification for building a powerful navy was to protect major maritime commercial interests. In his later writing, however, he concluded that the French need to maintain a first-class army to defend exposed land frontiers meant that it could never have overcome insular Britain, which, unhindered by having to maintain large land forces to protect home territory, could concentrate most of its resources on naval development. He also came to believe that factors other than a large merchant marine could justify investment in the construction of a substantial fleet.

---

[4] Mahan's apparent statement to the contrary in *Naval Strategy*, 11–2, must be read in relation to what he says elsewhere.

In addition to changes of mind over time that placed early and later views at odds, variation in the application of principles introduced at least the appearance of contradiction in Mahan's works. Mahan praised both circumspection and boldness, admired initiative even to the point of insubordination while insisting upon the fundamental importance of obedience and discipline, encouraged attentiveness to as well as disregard of logistical considerations, held that decisive fleet action was the highest goal of naval warfare yet on occasion lauded or recommended contrary courses of action, and recognized that the division of forces or bureaucratized administration was sometimes essential even while declaring his allegiance to the principles of concentration of force and unified responsibility. In these and other cases, Mahan pitted theory against elaboration, qualification, and exception in order to induce the strenuous mental exertion that was necessary to facilitate the generation of improved judgment. Mahan's writing thus was bound to be difficult because of tensions between its parts that were essential to the fulfillment of its pedagogical purpose.

Contradiction also occurred when Mahan explored the possible future geopolitical contexts of national grand strategy. He sometimes foretold an outcome that was the opposite of a prediction made earlier. This was a reflection of intellectual sophistication, not weakness. When Mahan engaged in punditry about the future as opposed to analysis about the distant past, what mattered most was not the accuracy of his prediction, but the rigor of his thought. The attitude of certainty that was attached to Mahan's speculative writing, therefore, was not about the infallibility of conclusions, but the integrity of the logic for a given set of assumptions. Moreover, Mahan's historically based policy analysis was a matter not so much of identifying trends and extending them, or of simple reasoning by analogy, but of applying judgment that had been well-schooled in the study of complex historical phenomena, with due appreciation for the bounded but still significant and possibly even decisive role that contingency could play. In sum, he did not reject contradiction, but rather embraced it, recognizing that its production was inherent to the intelligent consideration of what was a range of possibility, not a singular certainty yet to come.

Complexity, contingency, change, and contradiction in Mahan's texts made it difficult to perceive his sophisticated and nuanced conceptions of naval grand strategy and the art and science of command. On the other hand, his practical objectives of encouraging the construction of a much larger American navy—objectives that stood hand in hand with strong anti-isolationist and even imperialist views—and the basing of officer higher education upon the study of history rather than science or engineering were simple and constant and thus relatively easy to discern. Moreover, these propositions, which constituted Mahan's subtext in the "Influence of Sea Power" series and which were stated explicitly in the lesser works, were prone to conversion by careless reading or partisan debate into calls for American naval supremacy and advocacy of prescriptive strategic doctrine. Thus the substance of Mahan's text, which was hard to identify, let alone engage, was displaced not merely by the subtext but by corrupted understandings of that subtext.

To be sure, the polemical force of the first element of Mahan's actual subtext—the desirability of expanding the American navy—was well served by exaggeration. And it was in this form that Mahan's work had its greatest effect upon major events by moving public opinion in his own country and in modified form influencing the discussion of naval affairs in other maritime nations. The second element—history as the basis of officer education—became the stock in trade of war colleges. Although read only in small portions, if at all, Mahan's books could be presented as a testament to the value of historical training, the bulk of which could be provided by more up-to-date materials. The political and educational consequences of Mahan read as ideology or as a model of historically informed strategic theory were considerable and deserve the study that they have received. But although the reasoned substance of Mahan's text was overlooked and thus had little if any practical effect, his concepts of naval grand strategy and the art and science of command possess enough intellectual merit in their own right to justify serious consideration.

NAVAL SUPREMACY IN THE TWENTIETH CENTURY

Mahan's notion of twentieth-century naval supremacy being exercised by two or more states whose cooperation was not necessarily formalized was based on two sets of propositions. The first was that effective sea forces were expensive and the domestic political circumstances of industrial countries precluded any single power from spending enough to build and maintain a hegemonic navy. The second was that seaborne international trade offered benefits to more than one country, that two or more powers thus could have good reason to pool their resources to defend a mutually beneficial system of transoceanic exchange of goods, and that combined action based on shared economic interest could be enhanced by, but did not require the existence of, treaties. By viewing naval supremacy in terms of a transnational consortium, Mahan in effect abandoned the single nation-state as the basic unit of analysis, thus anticipating the work of later important historians.[5]

The concept of a transnational naval consortium protecting a large and growing system of international trade is broader and more flexible than the notion of naval supremacy as essential to any power desiring primacy in the international political system. Moreover, the proposition that tacit general understandings based upon economic and grand-strategic common interests could be the basis of significant great-power cooperative action offers a novel means of looking at the so-called Anglo-American "special relationship," connecting it to the general growth of international trade, as well as shared political heritage, language, and culture. Mahan's encouragement of friendship between the United States and Britain can thus be seen for what it was—namely, a policy recommendation that reflected his views on the nature of global political-economic developments and their consequences for national strategy, not merely the sentimental expressions of an Anglophile.[6]

Mahan's concept of a transnational naval consortium can be seen as occupying a position between nationalism and internationalism. Mahan recognized that parochial interests were bound to condition heavily the action of national governments. At the same time, however, he was convinced that because even the strongest great powers were incapable of unilaterally defending a worldwide system of maritime commerce, the requirements of national interest could dictate that two countries with substantial involvement in international trade should cooperate. Mahan also believed that there was a real possibility that fundamental cultural differences would provoke a cataclysmic conflict pitting Europe and possibly the United States on the one hand against a militant Asia on

---

[5] For example, see Immanuel Wallerstein, *The Modern World-System: Capitalist Agriculture and the Origins of the European World-Economy in the Sixteenth Century* (New York: Academic Press, 1976), and William H. McNeill, *The Pursuit of Power: Technology, Armed Force, and Society since A.D. 1000* (Chicago, Ill.: University of Chicago Press, 1982).

[6] For various aspects of Anglo-American relations, see Charles C. Colby, *North Atlantic Arena: Water Transport in the World Order* (Carbondale: Southern Illinois University Press, 1966); David Reynolds, *The Creation of the Anglo-American Alliance, 1937–1941: A Study of Competitive Co-operation* (Chapel Hill: University of North Carolina Press, 1982); Ian K. Steele, *The English Atlantic, 1675–1740: An Exploration of Communication and Community* (New York: Oxford University Press, 1986); and David Dimbleby and David Reynolds, *An Ocean Apart: The Relationship between Britain and America in the Twentieth Century* (New York: Random House, 1988).

the other, an eventuality that would require Western countries to put aside national differences without embracing the idea of world government. Mahanian political realism, in short, accorded national interest its due while also recognizing that there were other forces in play.

Mahan's transnational approach offers a fruitful way of reconsidering the naval history of the industrial age. Accounts of British and American naval power in the era of steam are always told as separate stories, of decline in the case of the former and rise in the case of the latter.[7] Naval history written from a transnational perspective, in contrast, might trace the fortunes of an Anglo-American naval consortium, in which the Royal Navy's slip to second place on the one hand, and the U.S. Navy's assumption of first place on the other, would matter insofar as relative status within the partnership was concerned but would not change the fact that the essential security of the international system of trade that was being defended was maintained consistently through cooperation. The main point of a naval history that covered both Britain and the United States, in other words, would not be about the progress of decrepitude in one instance and maturation of preeminence in the other, but the continuous viability of a two-party relationship that was expanded after 1945 to include the navies of other powers.

MAHAN, JOMINI, AND CLAUSEWITZ

Most historians believe that Mahan derived his approach to the art and science of command from the work of Jomini. Jomini codified Napoleonic military practice into a body of rules, which if not intended as absolutely unbreakable, were nevertheless regarded by their author as representing a firm guide to sound practice. The two watchwords of his writing, according to one recent authority, were "reductionism and prescription."[8] The association of Mahan and Jomini, based upon the supposedly Jominian thinking of Mahan's father and references to Jomini in his own writing, probably contributed much to the sense that

---

[7] For example, see George W. Baer, *One Hundred Years of Sea Power: The U.S. Navy, 1890–1990* (Stanford, Calif.: Stanford University Press, 1994); Kenneth J. Hagen, *This People's Navy: The Making of American Sea Power* (New York: Free Press, 1991); Paul M. Kennedy, *The Rise and Fall of British Naval Mastery* (New York: Charles Scribner's Sons, 1976); and Desmond Wettern, *The Decline of British Seapower* (London: Jane's, 1982).
[8] John Shy, "Jomini," in *Makers of Modern Strategy from Machiavelli to the Nuclear Age*, ed. Peter Paret (Princeton, N.J.: Princeton University Press, 1986), 172. See also Peter Paret, *Clausewitz and the State* (Oxford, U.K.: Clarendon, 1976), 204–5.

Alfred Thayer Mahan was mechanistic and doctrinaire. Dennis Hart Mahan, however, was anti-Jominian in his distrust of systematic theory in matters of command. And while Alfred Thayer Mahan attributed his method of critical commentary on historical narrative to Jomini and used his basic principles as the starting point for analysis, Mahan like his father rejected the notion that the essential nature of command in war could be encompassed by a system of rules.

In placing greater emphasis on art than on science when it came to the question of command in war, the Mahans resembled Clausewitz rather than Jomini. This was especially true with regard to attitude toward comprehensive theory. In a preface to an unpublished work that was the precursor to his famous *On War*, Clausewitz wrote

> There is no need today to labor the point that a scientific approach does not consist solely, or even mainly, in a complete system and a comprehensive doctrine. In the formal sense the present work contains no such system; instead of a complete theory it offers only material for one.
>
> Its scientific character consists in an attempt to investigate the essence of the phenomena of war and to indicate the links between these phenomena and the nature of their component parts. No logical conclusion has been avoided; but whenever the thread became too thin I have preferred to break it off and go back to the relevant phenomena of experience. Just as some plants bear fruit only if they don't shoot up too high, so in the practical arts the leaves and flowers of theory must be pruned and the plant kept close to its proper soil—experience.[9]

At bottom, Clausewitz, like the Mahans, believed that command had to be exercised in the face of uncertainty and thus required moral as well as intellectual qualities. He expressed his views in terms that were similar to those later used by the younger Mahan. In *On War*, the Prussian officer wrote that "since all information and assumptions are open to doubt, and with chance at work everywhere, the commander continually finds that things are not as he expected," and that the inflow of new information only made him "more, not less uncertain." He then

[9] Carl von Clausewitz, "To an Unpublished Manuscript on the Theory of War, Written between 1816 and 1818," in *On War*, ed. and trans. Michael Howard and Peter Paret (Princeton, N.J.: Princeton University Press, 1976), 61.

noted that "if the mind is to emerge unscathed from this relentless struggle with the unforeseen, two qualities are indispensable: first, an intellect that, even in the darkest hour, retains some glimmerings of the inner light which leads to truth; and second, the courage to follow this faint light wherever it may lead." Clausewitz explained that courage did not mean physical bravery, but rather "the courage to accept responsibility, courage in the face of a moral danger." "Looked at in this way," he went on to say, "the role of determination is to limit the agonies of doubt and the perils of hesitation when the motives for action are inadequate."[10]

Clausewitz's views on the limitations of theory, or what he called positive doctrine, and the concomitant necessity for a special kind of executive judgment resembled those of Mahan. "Given the nature of the subject," Clausewitz wrote in *On War*, "we must remind ourselves that it is simply not possible to construct a model for the art of war that can serve as a scaffolding on which the commander can rely for support at any time. Whenever he has to fall back on his innate talent, he will find himself outside of the model and in conflict with it; no matter how versatile the code, the situation will always lead to the consequences we have already alluded to: *talent and genius operate outside the rules, and theory conflicts with practice*."[11] "The influence of theoretical truths on practical life," Clausewitz wrote later in *On War*, "is always exerted more through critical analysis than through doctrine."[12] To this he later added the warning that "one should never use elaborate scientific guidelines as if they were a kind of truth machine."[13]

Clausewitz maintained that theory could be "a guide to anyone who wants to learn about war from books; it will light his way, ease his progress, train his judgment, and help him to avoid pitfalls." But he then warned that while theory was "meant to educate the mind of the future commander, or, more accurately, to guide him in his self-education," it was "not to accompany him to the battlefield." The reason for this assertion was because while "knowledge in war *is very simple*, being concerned with so few subjects, and only with their final results," this did "not make its application easy." The nature of the knowledge required to facilitate application "cannot be forcibly pro-

[10] Clausewitz, *On War*, book 1, chap. 3, 102–3.
[11] Ibid., book 2, chap. 2, 140. Italics in the original.
[12] Ibid., chap. 5, 156.
[13] Ibid., 168.

duced by an apparatus of scientific formulas and mechanics; it can only be gained through a talent for judgment, and by the application of accurate judgment to the observation of man and matter."[14]

Judgment was best educated by actual combat experience, but given the near impossibility of obtaining such in peacetime,[15] Clausewitz, as Mahan was to do later, placed his confidence in the next best thing, namely, the study of detailed critical history, which he viewed as a form of experience. Clausewitz maintained in *On War* that "the critic must naturally frequently refer to military history, for in the art of war experience counts more than any amount of abstract truths."[16] He later observed that "historical examples clarify everything and also provide the best kind of proof in the empirical sciences," but that the "use made of them by theorists normally not only leaves the reader dissatisfied but even irritates his intelligence." Clausewitz's ideal was detailed narrative that was informed by theoretical understanding, produced by someone with both highly developed scholarly abilities and "personal experience of war," that could serve as the basis of teaching the "art of war entirely by historical examples."[17]

Clausewitz was convinced that proper study would enhance the ability of a commander to learn from experience. "The knowledge needed by a senior commander," he wrote, "is distinguished by the fact that it can only be attained by a special talent, through the medium of reflection, study and thought: an intellectual instinct which extracts the essence from the phenomena of life, as a bee sucks honey from a flower. In addition to study and reflection, life itself serves as a source."[18] "Knowledge," Clausewitz added shortly thereafter, "must be so absorbed into the mind that it almost ceases to exist in a separate, objective way. . . . Continual change and the need to respond to it compels the commander to carry the whole intellectual apparatus of his knowledge within him. He must always be ready to bring forth the appropriate decision. By total assimilation with his mind and life, the commander's knowledge must be transformed into a genuine capability."[19]

Clausewitz and the Mahans devoted much of their professional careers to the education of officers, and their approaches to this task were

---

[14] Ibid., 141, 146. Italics in the original.
[15] Ibid., 122; and Mahan, *Naval Strategy*, 297.
[16] Clausewitz, *On War*, book 2, chap. 5, 164.
[17] Ibid., chap. 6, 170–4.
[18] Ibid., chap. 2, 146.
[19] Ibid., 147.

fundamentally the same. All three regarded war as a complex and contingent phenomenon whose nature could not be encompassed by any system of theory. They thus believed that the purpose of instruction about decision-making was to produce a mindset that was better prepared to learn from actual operational experience, and that the resulting synthesis of peacetime preparation and war-learning would be an invaluable and possibly decisively important asset. Given this, the three men regarded the efficacious engagement with a portion of practical reality to be more important than the building of a whole system whose construction necessarily required simplification that compromised the veracious representation of war operations. The incompleteness of their writing from a theoretical standpoint can thus be seen as inherent to their concern for authenticity, not an oversight.

Mahan finished the last installment of the "Influence of Sea Power" series before what is believed to have been his first encounter with the writings of Clausewitz,[20] which would mean that the similarity indicated by the preceding discussion may be attributed to independent discovery by Mahan, though he was born several years after Clausewitz's death. There is a suggestive use of distinctly Clausewitzian terminology—the term "friction"—in Mahan's biography of Nelson,[21] but whether this came directly from translated editions of Clausewitz's work[22] or indirectly through either Dennis Hart Mahan or Stephen Luce is impossible to say.[23] In any case, Mahan's outlook was identical

---

[20] For Mahan's late familiarity with (possibly as early as 1908, certainly in 1910) and admiration of Clausewitz, see Mahan to Raymond P. Rodgers, 4 March 1911, in *The Letters and Papers of Alfred Thayer Mahan*, ed. Robert Seager II and Doris Maguire, 3 vols. (Annapolis, Md.: Naval Institute Press, 1977), iii: 394; and Captain W. D. Puleston, *Mahan: The Life and Work of Captain Alfred Thayer Mahan* (New Haven, Conn.: Yale University Press, 1939), 293–6.

[21] Captain A. T. Mahan, *The Life of Nelson: The Embodiment of the Sea Power of Great Britain*, 2 vols. (Boston: Little, Brown, 1897), ii: 129. For the suggestion that Mahan was familiar with Clausewitz in the 1890s, see Christopher Bassford, *Clausewitz in English: The Reception of Clausewitz in Britain and America, 1815–1945* (New York: Oxford University Press, 1994), 95.

[22] The first English-language edition of *On War* appeared in 1873, for which see Bassford, *Clausewitz in English*, 56–7.

[23] For the certainty that Rear Admiral Stephen Luce was familiar with Clausewitz's work in the 1890s, which strongly suggests that Mahan would also have known of it, see Stephen B. Luce, "Stonewall Jackson and the American Civil War," *The Critic* 34 (January 1899), 65–7, reprinted in *The Writings of Stephen B. Luce*, ed. John D. Hayes and John B. Hattendorf, (Newport, R.I.: Naval War College Press, 1975), 107. For the possibility that Dennis Hart Mahan could have known about the substance of Clausewitz's writing, particularly with regard to the concept of "friction," through a long summary of *On War* published in 1835 in the *Metropolitan Magazine* in Great Britain and the *Military and Naval Magazine of the United States*, see Bassford, *Clausewitz in English*, 37–8.

to that of Clausewitz about things that were central to each other's thought. A Jominian by casual confession and to a degree in form, he was in substance, whether by direct or indirect inheritance or coincidence, a Clausewitzian.

COMMAND AND HISTORY

The outcomes of the protracted great wars of the twentieth century were to a large degree determined by the capacity of the victors to develop overwhelming quantitative superiorities in men and matériel. In the First World War, Mahan's own U.S. Navy expanded by a factor of ten; in the Second World War, it expanded by a factor of twenty. Although the high command was exercised by seasoned professionals, the need to produce numerous hostilities-only officers prompted the writing of handbooks that emphasized the technical and human relations aspects of leadership and discussed operational decision-making only briefly and in highly prescriptive and reductionist formats.[24] It was this body of literature, and not the works of Mahan, that formed the primary written basis for the command culture of the U.S. Navy.[25]

During the Second World War, unlike in the First, the U.S. Navy fought a succession of major fleet actions. Participants in these battles were compelled to learn their trade in real combat under difficult conditions. The encounters in the Solomon Islands were especially bitter contests, often against superior forces, the experience of which for some generated a concept of command that echoed the views of Mahan. "Decentralization," wrote Admiral Arleigh Burke, who led a destroyer

---

[24] U.S. Naval War College, *Sound Military Decision*, ed. Captain Frank M. Snyder (Annapolis, Md.: Naval Institute Press, 1942); Arthur A. Ageton, *The Naval Officer's Guide* (New York: Whittlesey House, McGraw-Hill, 1943); and Harley F. Cope, *Command at Sea: A Guide for the Naval Officer* (New York: Norton, 1943). See also Office of the Superintendent, U.S. Naval Academy, *Naval Leadership with Some Hints to Junior Officers and Others* (Annapolis, Md.: United States Naval Institute, 1924); and Superintendent, U.S. Naval Academy, *Naval Leadership* (Annapolis, Md.: U.S. Naval Institute, 1949).
[25] For the nonuse of Mahan by naval war colleges by World War II, see Herbert Rosinski, "Mahan and World War II," in *The Development of Naval Thought: Essays by Herbert Rosinski*, ed. B. Mitchell Simpson III, (Newport, R.I.: Naval War College Press, 1977), 20–1.

squadron during the Solomon Islands campaign and was later to become chief of naval operations,

> means we offer officers the opportunity to rise to positions of
> responsibility, of decision, of identity and stature—if they want it,
> and as soon as they can take it.
>   We believe in command, not staff. We believe we have "real"
> things to do. The Navy believes in putting a man in a position
> with a job to do, and let him do it—give him hell if he does not
> perform—but to be a man in his own name. We decentralize and
> capitalize on the capabilities of our individual people rather than
> centralize and make automatons of them. This builds that essen-
> tial pride of service and sense of accomplishment.[26]

Burke's remarks exemplified the leadership values of his generation, the
hold of which, however, was bound to weaken as veterans of the war
retired and were replaced by younger men who lacked both direct experience and the kind of historical instruction called for by Mahan.
    A good deal of what Mahan wrote about the age of sail has been su-
perseded by modern scholarship.[27] Moreover, during the century that
has elapsed since the debut of *The Influence of Sea Power upon History*,
two world wars have provided the record of great campaigns between
first-rate powers fought with industrial matériel that did not exist during Mahan's lifetime. Not only is there a need for a new comprehensive
international history of preindustrial navies, but Mahan's "naval warfare
of the future" is now the past, and recourse to accounts of the great conflicts between France and Britain can no longer be justified as Mahan
did—on the grounds that it was the only "history which can be quoted
as decisive in its teaching."[28] But although perhaps obsolete as reliable
narrative or complete analysis, Mahan's concern with the effects of
complexity and contingency and his belief that history represented a

---

[26] Admiral Arleigh Burke to Rear Admiral Walter G. Schindler on 14 May 1958, quoted
by David Rosenberg in *The Chiefs of Naval Operations*, ed. Robert William Love, Jr. (Annapolis, Md.: Naval Institute Press, 1980), 287. See also [David] Alan Rosenberg, "Admiral Arleigh A. Burke," in *Men of War: Great Naval Leaders of World War II*, ed. Stephen
Howarth (London: Weidenfeld and Nicolson, 1992), 506–27.
[27] A select list of relatively recent major works on the period covered by the "Influence of
Sea Power" series is given in the bibliography.
[28] Mahan, *Influence of Sea Power upon History*, 2.

form of experience that when presented properly could be assimilated as such make his works both a source of provocative methodological suggestion[29] and a worthy subject of serious philosophical discussion.[30]

But above all, Mahan's treatment of the art and science of command has retained much of its applicability because the U.S. Navy is no longer led by the combat veterans of a major conflict and because the conditions of prolonged general peace have stimulated the growth of the same kind of problems, as well as adding new ones with similar effects, that had prompted Mahan to write about the education of naval officers in the first place. The size and complication of late-twentieth-century military bureaucracy, the involvement of officers with the armaments industry in the protracted process of development and procurement of new weapons, the integration of the operational decision-making of the separate services, the difficulties of adjusting military culture and practice to match those of a rapidly changing larger society, and the vulnerability of military leaders to both justifiable and unjustifiable attacks in the news media have all disfavored the development of leadership characterized by rapidity of action, decisiveness, and a willingness to assume responsibility. Engaging Mahan's thinking about the nature and role of naval executive function, therefore, may serve as a reminder of first principles and at least mitigate the effect of tendencies detrimental to effective command in war.

Mahan's concept of naval leadership ability and its development has broader implications. Recent advances in computation and communications have encouraged the emphasis of access to ever-larger quantities of information without commensurate concern for the quality of judgment required to make practical sense of data pools of such unprecedented size and complexity. The "information revolution" has

---

[29] Mahan's approach to the investigation of the past might profitably be considered in relation to ideas being put forward by historians attracted to the utility of chaos and complexity theory, for which see Donald M. McCloskey, "History, Differential Equations, and the Problem of Narration," *History and Theory* 30 (1991), 21–36; and Roger Beaumont, *War, Chaos, and History* (Westport, Conn.: Praeger, 1995).

[30] See Ludwig Wittgenstein, *Philosophical Investigations*, trans. G.E.M. Anscombe, 3rd ed. (New York: Macmillan, 1958), 227e; R. G. Collingwood, *The Idea of History* (Oxford, U.K.: Clarendon, 1946), esp. 282–315; R. G. Collingwood, "Are History and Science Different Kinds of Knowledge?" in *Essays in the Philosophy of History*, ed. William Debbins (New York: McGraw-Hill, 1966), 23–33; *Essays in Political Philosophy*, ed. David Boucher (Oxford, U.K.: Clarendon, 1995), esp. 1–2, 38–9, 171–4; Alan Donagan, *The Later Philosophy of R. G. Collingwood* (Oxford, U.K.: Clarendon, 1962), esp. 87–91, 192–6, 214–22; and William H. Dray, *History as Re-Enactment* (Oxford, U.K.: Clarendon, 1995).

transformed not only the conduct of military operations but the direction of private economic and public governmental activity at all levels. In the latter cases, the consequences of leadership failure do not involve loss of life as in war but are nonetheless dire enough to induce fear sufficient to promote indecisiveness. Mahan's emphasis on the development of a powerful and flexible intelligence that was buttressed by moral strength and his no less equal concern with the integration of these characteristics with technical ability define essential qualities of effective command under modern circumstances of contingency and danger. For this reason, his approach to teaching is applicable in fundamental ways to the higher education of leadership in the civilian as well as the military world.

To engage Mahan's views on command is to grapple with the problem posed by the mysterious dynamics of human cognition and learning in their relation to action that requires volition. Mahan believed that officers should possess a temperament capable of asserting judgment rapidly in the face of great uncertainty and other difficult conditions. Such an artistic mentality, however, had to be joined to engineering and administrative capability that worked in terms of certain knowledge and the consistent application of absolute rules. Mahan was convinced that in teaching war leadership, much depended upon the maintenance of a proper balance between these conflicting propensities, with the emphasis placed upon art rather than science. Theory alone was inherently prescriptive and reductionist and thus posed the danger of reinforcing rather than offsetting science. While history provided weaker leverage from the standpoint of pure logic, it was also less restrictive and thus left room for the play of imagination that is characteristic of human creativity. Mahan therefore insisted that the study of history serve as the primary agent of advanced education for those charged with the task of directing what was technologically and bureaucratically the most complex institution of his time, and ours.

Bibliography

MAJOR WORKS OF DENNIS HART MAHAN

Mahan, D. H. *A Complete Treatise on Field Fortification with General Outlines of the Principles Regulating the Arrangement, the Attack, and the Defence of Permanent Works*. New York: Greenwood, 1968. First published in 1836.

——. *An Elementary Treatise on Advanced-Guard, Out-Post, and Detachment Service of Troops: and the Manner of Posting and Handling Them in Presence of an Enemy intended as a Supplement to the System of Tactics. Adopted for the Military Service of the United States, and Especially for the Use of Officers of Militia and Volunteers*. New Orleans: Bloomfield and Steel, 1861. First published 1847. Microfiche edition, Louisville, Ky.: Lost Cause Press, 1979.

——. *Summary of the Course of Permanent Fortification and of the Attack and Defence of Permanent Works, for the Use of the Cadets of the U.S. Military Academy*. Richmond: West & Johnson, 1863. First published 1850. Microfiche edition, Louisville, Ky.: Lost Cause Press, 1979.

——. *Advanced-Guard, Out-Post, and Detachment Service of Troops, with the Essential Principles of Strategy, and Grand Tactics, for the Use of Officers of the Militia and Volunteers*. New York: John Wiley, 1863.

EARLY WORKS OF ALFRED THAYER MAHAN

Mahan, Commander A. T. "Naval Education." *United States Naval Institute Proceedings* 5 (December 1879): 345–76.

Mahan, A. T. *The Gulf and Inland Waters.* The Navy in the Civil War, vol. 3. New York: Charles Scribner's Sons, 1883.

Mahan, A. T. "Fleet Battle Tactics." Lecture (1886), Record Group 14, Naval War College Archives, Newport, R.I. Courtesy of Professor John Hattendorf.

THE "INFLUENCE OF SEA POWER" SERIES

Mahan, Alfred Thayer. *The Influence of Sea Power upon History, 1660–1783.* Boston: Little, Brown, 1890.

Mahan, Captain A. T. *The Influence of Sea Power upon the French Revolution and Empire, 1793–1812.* 2 vols. Boston: Little, Brown, 1892.

Mahan, Captain A. T. *The Life of Nelson: The Embodiment of the Sea Power of Great Britain.* 2 vols. Boston: Little, Brown, 1897.

Mahan, Captain A. T. *Sea Power in Its Relations to the War of 1812.* 2 vols. Boston: Little, Brown, 1905.

LESSER WORKS

Mahan, Captain A. T. *Admiral Farragut.* Great Commanders. New York: D. Appleton, 1897.

Mahan, Captain A. T. *The Interest of America in Sea Power, Present and Future.* Boston: Little, Brown, 1897.

Mahan, Alfred T. *Lessons of the War with Spain and Other Articles.* Boston: Little, Brown, 1899.

Mahan, A. T. *The Problem of Asia and Its Effect upon International Policies.* Boston: Little, Brown, 1900.

Mahan, Captain A. T. *The Story of the War in South Africa 1899–1900.* New York: Greenwood, 1968. First published 1900.

Mahan, A. T. *Types of Naval Officers Drawn from the History of the British Navy; With Some Account of the Conditions of Naval Warfare at the Beginning of the Eighteenth Century, and of Its Subsequent Development during the Sail Period.* Boston: Little, Brown, 1901.

Mahan, A. T. *Retrospect and Prospect: Studies in International Relations Naval and Political.* London: Sampson Low, Marston, 1902.

Mahan, Captain A. T. *Some Neglected Aspects of War.* Boston: Little, Brown, 1907.

Mahan, Capt. A. T. *From Sail to Steam: Recollections of Naval Life.* New York: Harper and Brothers, 1907.

Mahan, Captain A. T. *Naval Administration and Warfare: Some General Principles with Other Essays.* Boston: Little, Brown, 1908.

Mahan, A. T. *The Harvest Within: Thoughts on the Life of a Christian.* Boston: Little, Brown, 1909.

Mahan, A. T. *The Interest of America in International Conditions*. Boston: Little, Brown, 1910.

Mahan, A. T. *Naval Strategy*. Boston: Little, Brown, 1911.

Mahan, A. T. *Armaments and Arbitration, or The Place of Force in the International Relations of States*. New York: Harper, 1912.

Mahan, A. T. *The Major Operations of the Navies in the War of American Independence*. Boston: Little, Brown, 1913. Revised version of A. T. Mahan, "Major Operations of the Royal Navy, 1762–1783," chap. 31 in *The Royal Navy: A History from the Earliest Times to the Present*, 7 vols., ed. William Laird Clowes, vol. 3, 353–564. New York: AMS, 1966. First published 1897–1903.

BIOGRAPHIES

Gilliam, B. M. "The World of Captain Mahan." Ph.D. dissertation, Princeton University, 1961.

Griess, Thomas Everett. "Dennis Hart Mahan: West Point Professor and Advocate of Military Professionalism, 1830–1871." Ph.D. dissertation, Duke University, 1969.

Levy, Morris. "Alfred Thayer Mahan and United States Foreign Policy." Ph.D. dissertation, New York University, 1965.

Puleston, W. D. *Mahan: The Life and Work of Captain Alfred Thayer Mahan*. New Haven, Conn.: Yale University Press, 1939.

Seager, Robert, II. *Alfred Thayer Mahan: The Man and His Letters*. Annapolis, Md.: Naval Institute Press, 1977.

Seager, Robert, II, and Doris D. Maguire, eds. *Letters and Papers of Alfred Thayer Mahan*. 3 vols. Annapolis, Md.: Naval Institute Press, 1975.

Taylor, Charles Carlisle. *The Life of Admiral Mahan: Naval Philosopher*. New York: George H. Doran, 1920.

Turk, Richard W. *The Ambiguous Relationship: Theodore Roosevelt and Alfred Thayer Mahan*. New York: Greenwood, 1987.

CRITICAL BOOKS, ANTHOLOGIES, AND SOURCE GUIDES

Hattendorf, John B. *Register of the Papers of Alfred T. Mahan*. Newport, R.I.: Naval War College, 1987.

———. *Mahan on Naval Strategy: Selections from the Writings of Rear Admiral Alfred Thayer Mahan*. Annapolis, Md.: Naval Institute Press, 1991.

Hattendorf, John B., and Lynn C. Hattendorf, comps. *A Bibliography of the Works of Alfred Thayer Mahan*. Newport, R.I.: Naval War College, 1986.

Kirkham, George. *The Books and Articles of Alfred Thayer Mahan*. New York: Ballou, 1919.

Livezey, William E. *Mahan on Sea Power*, rev. ed. Norman: University of Oklahoma Press, 1980. First published 1947.

Westcott, Allan. *Mahan on Naval Warfare: Selections from the Writings of Rear Admiral Alfred T. Mahan*. Boston: Little, Brown, 1941.

CRITICAL ARTICLES

Albion, Robert G., and Ralph Earle. "Alfred Thayer Mahan," in *Makers of Naval Tradition*, ed. Robert G. Albion and Ralph Earle, 228–46. New York: Ginn, 1925.

Baer, George. "Under the Influence: A Hundred Years and Around the World," in *The Influence of History on Mahan: The Proceedings of a Conference Marking the Centenary of Alfred Thayer Mahan's "The Influence of Sea Power upon History, 1660–1783,"* ed. John B. Hattendorf, 203–8. Newport, R.I.: Naval War College Press, 1991.

Brendt, Robert. "Mahan—Mariner or Misfit?" *United States Naval Institute Proceedings* 92 (1966): 92–103.

Carpenter, Ronald H. "Admiral Mahan, 'Narrative Fidelity,' and the Japanese Attack on Pearl Harbor: The Rhetorical Interaction between Discourse and Corroborative Events," in *Naval History: The Seventh Symposium of the U.S. Naval Academy*, ed. William B. Cogar, 195–211. Wilmington, Del.: Scholarly Resources, 1988.

———. "Alfred Thayer Mahan's Style in History as a Persuasive Paramessage: A Subtle Impress" and "Alfred Thayer Mahan as Opinion Leader of the Japanese Attack on Pearl Harbor: Narrative Fidelity with Fact," in *History as Rhetoric: Style, Narrative, and Persuasion*, ed. Ronald H. Carpenter, 107–80. Columbia: University of South Carolina Press, 1995.

Crowl, Philip A. "Alfred Thayer Mahan: The Naval Historian," in *Makers of Modern Strategy from Machiavelli to the Nuclear Age*, ed. Peter Paret, 444–77. Princeton, N.J.: Princeton University Press, 1986.

Davis, George T. "Mahan the Prophet" and "Mahan's Disciples," in *A Navy Second to None: The Development of Modern American Naval Policy*, 72–85, 135–49. New York: Harcourt Brace, 1940.

Downs, Robert B. "Ruling the Waves: Alfred T. Mahan's *The Influence of Sea Power upon History*," in *Books that Changed America*, 110–22. New York: Macmillan, 1970.

Dudley, William S. "Alfred Thayer Mahan on the War of 1812," in *The Influence of History on Mahan: The Proceedings of a Conference Marking the Centenary of Alfred Thayer Mahan's "The Influence of Sea Power upon History, 1660–1783,"* ed. John B. Hattendorf, 141–54. Newport, R.I.: Naval War College Press, 1991.

Duncan, Francis. "Mahan—Historian with a Purpose," *United States Naval Institute Proceedings* 83 (May 1957): 498–503.

Field, James. "Alfred Thayer Mahan Speaks for Himself," *Naval War College Review* 29 (fall 1976): 47–60.

Gat, Azar. "From Sail to Steam: Naval Theory and the Military Parallel, 1882–1914," in *The Development of Military Thought: The Nineteenth Century*, 173–225. Oxford, U.K.: Clarendon, 1992.

Glick, Edward Bernhard. "The Influence of a Historian on History," *Military Review* (April 1972): 31–4.

Godfrey, Jack E. "'Mahan': The Man, His Writings and Philosophy," *Naval War College Review* 21 (March 1969): 59–68.

Gooch, John. "Maritime Command: Mahan and Corbett," in *Seapower and Strategy*, ed. Colin S. Gray and Roger W. Barnett, 27–46. Annapolis, Md.: Naval Institute Press, 1989.

Gough, Barry M. "The Influence of History on Mahan," in *The Influence of History on Mahan: The Proceedings of a Conference Marking the Centenary of Alfred Thayer Mahan's "The Influence of Sea Power upon History, 1660–1783,"* ed. John B. Hattendorf, 7–23. Newport, R.I.: Naval War College Press, 1991.

Hacker, Louis M. "The Incendiary Mahan: A Biography," *Scribner's Monthly* 95 (April 1934): 263–8, 311–20.

Hagen, Kenneth J. "The Apotheosis of Mahan: American Naval Strategy, 1889–1922," in *Navies and Global Defense: Theories and Strategy*, ed. Keith Neilson and Elizabeth Jane Errington, 92–115. Westport, Conn.: Praeger, 1995.

Hattendorf, John B. "Alfred Thayer Mahan and His Strategic Thought," in *Maritime Strategy and the Balance of Power: Britain and America in the Twentieth Century*, ed. John B. Hattendorf and Robert S. Jordan, 83–94. New York: St. Martin's, 1989.

———. "Alfred Thayer Mahan and American Naval Theory," in *Navies and Global Defense: Theories and Strategy*, ed. Keith Neilson and Elizabeth Jane Errington, 51–92. Westport, Conn.: Praeger, 1995.

Hayes, John D. "The Writings of Alfred Thayer Mahan," *Military Affairs* 19 (winter 1955): 186–96.

Hughes, Wayne P. "Mahan, Tactics and Principles of Strategy," in *The Influence of History on Mahan: The Proceedings of a Conference Marking the Centenary of Alfred Thayer Mahan's "The Influence of Sea Power upon History, 1660–1783,"* ed. John B. Hattendorf, 25–36. Newport, R.I.: Naval War College Press, 1991.

Karsten, Peter. "Mahan Reconsidered," in *The Naval Aristocracy: The Golden Age of Annapolis and the Emergence of Modern American Navalism*, 326–52. New York: Free Press, 1972.

Keegan, John. "Why Are Britain's Great Naval Historians Americans?" *Naval History* 1 (April 1987): 7–11.

Kennedy, Paul. "Mahan versus Mackinder: Two Interpretations of British Sea Power," in *Strategy and Diplomacy 1870–1945: Eight Studies*, 43–85. London: Fontana, 1984.

Langer, William L. "The New Navalism," in *The Diplomacy of Imperialism 1890–1902*, 415–44. 2nd ed. New York: Alfred A. Knopf, 1972.

LaFeber, Walter. "A Note on the 'Mercantilistic Imperialism' of Alfred Thayer Mahan," *Mississippi Valley Historical Review* 48 (March 1962): 674–85.

Leslie, Reo N., Jr. "Christianity and the Evangelist for Sea Power: The Religion of Alfred Thayer Mahan," in *The Influence of History on Mahan: The Proceedings of a Conference Marking the Centenary of Alfred Thayer Mahan's "The Influence of Sea*

Power upon History, 1660–1783," ed. John B. Hattendorf, 127–39. Newport, R.I.: Naval War College Press, 1991.

Lewis, Charles L. "Alfred Thayer Mahan," in *Famous American Naval Officers,* 255–74. Boston: L. C. Page, 1924.

Maurer, John H. "Mahan on World Politics and Strategy: The Approach of the First World War, 1904–1914, in *The Influence of History on Mahan: The Proceedings of a Conference Marking the Centenary of Alfred Thayer Mahan's "The Influence of Sea Power upon History, 1660–1783,"* ed. John B. Hattendorf, 157–76. Newport, R.I.: Naval War College Press, 1991.

Mead, Lucia A. "The Fallacies of Captain Mahan," *Arena* 40 (September 1908): 163–70.

Moll, Kenneth. "A. T. Mahan, American Historian," *Military Affairs* 28 (fall 1963): 131–40.

O'Connell, Robert L. "Upon This Rock: The Technological Revolution and the Prophet Mahan," in *Sacred Vessels: The Cult of the Battleship and the Rise of the U.S. Navy,* 39–71. Boulder, Colo.: Westview, 1991.

Pratt, Julius W. "The 'Large Policy' of 1898," *Mississippi Valley Historical Review* 19 (September 1932): 219–42.

———. "Alfred Thayer Mahan" in *The Marcus W. Jernegan Essays in American Historiography,* ed. William T. Hutchinson, 207–26. Chicago, Ill.: University of Chicago Press, 1937.

Puleston, William D. "A Reexamination of Mahan's Concept of Seapower," *United States Naval Institute Proceedings* 66 (September 1940): 1229–36.

Quester, George. "Mahan and American Naval Thought since 1914," in *The Influence of History on Mahan: The Proceedings of a Conference Marking the Centenary of Alfred Thayer Mahan's "The Influence of Sea Power upon History, 1660–1783,"* ed. John B. Hattendorf, 177–95. Newport, R.I.: Naval War College Press, 1991.

Reitzel, William. "Mahan on the Use of the Sea," *Naval War College Review* 25 (May–June 1973): 73–82.

Reynolds, Clark G. "Captain Mahan, Thalassocratic Determinist," in *History and the Sea: Essays on Maritime Strategies,* 66–76. Columbia: University of South Carolina Press, 1989.

———. "Mahan, Russia, and the Next 100 Years," in *The Influence of History on Mahan: The Proceedings of a Conference Marking the Centenary of Alfred Thayer Mahan's "The Influence of Sea Power upon History, 1660–1783,"* ed. John B. Hattendorf, 197–201. Newport, R.I.: Naval War College Press, 1991.

Roosevelt, Theodore. "The Great Public Servant," *Outlook* 109 (13 January 1915): 85–6.

Rosinski, Herbert. "Command at Sea" and "Mahan and World War II: A Commentary from the United States," in *The Development of Naval Thought: Essays by Herbert Rosinski,* ed. B. Mitchell Simpson III, 1–40. Newport, R.I.: Naval War College Press, 1977.

Schurman, Donald M. "The American: Admiral Alfred," in *The Education of a Navy: The Development of British Naval Strategic Thought, 1867–1914,* 60–82. Chicago, Ill.: University of Chicago Press, 1965.

———. "An Historian and the Sublime Aspects of the Naval Profession," in *Dreadnought to Polaris: Maritime Strategy since Mahan*, ed. A. M. J. Hyatt, 1–11. Toronto: Copp Clark; Annapolis, Md.: Naval Institute Press, 1973.

———. "Mahan Revisited," in *Maritime Strategy and the Balance of Power: Britain and America in the Twentieth Century*, ed. John B. Hattendorf and Robert S. Jordan, 95–109. New York: St. Martin's, 1989.

Seager, Robert, II. "Alfred Thayer Mahan: Christian Expansionist, Navalist, and Historian," in *Admirals of the New Steel Navy: Makers of the American Naval Tradition, 1880–1930*, ed. James C. Bradford, 24–72. Annapolis, Md.: Naval Institute Press, 1990.

Slick, Bernard. "Mahan: The Influence of a Historian on History," *Military Review* 52 (April 1972): 31–4.

Sprout, Harold, and Margaret Sprout. "Alfred Thayer Mahan: Sea Power and the New Manifest Destiny (1889–1897)," in *The Rise of American Naval Power, 1776–1918*, 202–22. Princeton, N.J.: Princeton University Press, 1939.

Sprout, Margaret Tuttle. "Mahan: Evangelist of Sea Power," in *Makers of Modern Strategy: Military Thought from Machiavelli to Hitler*, ed. Edward Mead Earle, 415–45. Princeton, N.J.: Princeton University Press, 1941.

Weigley, Russell. "The Founding of American Strategic Studies: Dennis Hart Mahan and Henry Wager Halleck" and "A Strategy of Sea Power and Empire: Stephen B. Luce and Alfred Thayer Mahan," in *The American Way of War: A History of United States Military Strategy and Policy*, 77–91, 167–91. New York: Macmillan, 1973.

West, Richard. "Mahan Turns Naval Philosopher," "Mentor to Imperialists," "Mahan on the War Board," and "Triumph of Mahan," in *Admirals of American Empire: The Combined Story of George Dewey, Alfred Thayer Mahan, Winfield Scott Schley, and William Thomas Sampson*, 81–97, 146–62, 211–22, 303–23. Indianapolis, Ind.: Bobbs-Merrill, 1948.

RELATED MAJOR WORKS OF STRATEGIC HISTORY BY OTHERS

Castex, Admiral Raoul. *Strategic Theories*. Ed. and trans. by Eugenia C. Kiesling. Annapolis, Md.: Naval Institute Press, 1994. First published as *Théories stratégiques*, 5 vols., 1931–9.

von Clausewitz, Carl. *On War*. Ed. and trans. by Michael Howard and Peter Paret. Princeton, N.J.: Princeton University Press, 1976. First published 1832.

Colomb, Rear-Admiral P. H. *Naval Warfare: Its Ruling Principles and Practice Historically Treated*. London: W. H. Allen, 1891.

Corbett, Julian S. *Some Principles of Maritime Strategy*. Ed. by Eric J. Grove. Annapolis, Md.: Naval Institute Press, 1988. First published 1911.

Jomini, Baron Antoine. *The Art of War*. Trans. by G. H. Mendell and W. P. Craighill. Philadelphia: J. B. Lippincott, 1862. Reprinted New York: Greenwood Press, n.d.

Richmond, Admiral Sir Herbert. *Statesmen and Sea Power*. Oxford, U.K.: Clarendon, 1946.

Roskill, Captain S. W. *The Strategy of Sea Power: Its Development and Application*. London: Collins, 1962.

RELATED MAJOR WORKS ON COMMAND

Ageton, Arthur A. *The Naval Officer's Guide*. New York: McGraw-Hill, 1943.

Cope, Harley F. *Command at Sea*, New York: Norton, 1943.

van Creveld, Martin. *Command in War*. Cambridge, Mass.: Harvard University Press, 1985.

Grenfell, Commander Russell. *The Art of the Admiral*. London: Faber and Faber, 1937.

Nye, Roger H. *The Challenge of Command: Reading for Military Excellence*. Wayne, N.J.: Avery Publishing Group, 1986.

Roskill, Captain S. W. *The Art of Leadership*. London: Collins, 1964.

U.S. Naval Academy, Office of the Superintendent. *Naval Leadership with Some Hints to Junior Officers and Others*. Annapolis, Md.: U.S. Naval Institute, 1924.

———. *Naval Leadership*, 2nd ed. Annapolis, Md.: U.S. Naval Institute, 1959.

U.S. Naval War College. *Sound Military Decision: U.S. Naval War College*. Ed. by Captain Frank M. Snyder. Annapolis, Md.: Naval Institute Press, 1992. First published 1942.

SELECTED POST-MAHAN ACCOUNTS OF THE PERIOD COVERED BY THE "INFLUENCE OF SEA POWER" SERIES

Baugh, Daniel A. "The Politics of British Naval Failure, 1775–1777." *The American Neptune* 54 (fall 1992): 221–46.

Cormack, William S. *Revolution and Political Conflict in the French Navy, 1789–1794*. Cambridge, U.K.: Cambridge University Press, 1995.

Dull, John. *The French Navy and American Independence: A Study of Arms and Diplomacy, 1774–1787*. Princeton, N.J.: Princeton University Press, 1975.

Ehrman, John. *The Navy in the War of William III: Its State and Direction*. Cambridge, U.K.: Cambridge University Press, 1953.

Glete, Jan. *Navies and Nations: Warships, Navies and State Building in Europe and America, 1500–1860*. 2 vols. Stockholm: Almqvist and Wiksell International, 1993.

Lavery, Brian. *The Arming and Fitting of English Ships of War, 1600–1815*. Annapolis, Md.: Naval Institute Press, 1987.

———. *Nelson's Navy: The Ships, Men and Organisation, 1793–1815*. Annapolis, Md.: Naval Institute Press, 1989.

Marcus, G. J. *The Age of Nelson: The Royal Navy, 1793–1815*. New York: Viking, 1971.

Muir, Rory. *Britain and the Defeat of Napoleon, 1807–1815*. New Haven, Conn.: Yale University Press, 1996.

Smith, Gene A. *"For the Purposes of Defense": The Politics of the Jeffersonian Gunboat Program*. Newark, N.J.: University of Delaware Press, 1995.

Stagg, J. C. A. *Mr. Madison's War: Politics, Diplomacy, and Warfare in the Early American Republic, 1783–1830*. Princeton, N.J.: Princeton University Press, 1983.

Symcox, Geoffrey. *The Crisis of French Sea Power, 1688–1697: From the Guerre d'Escadre to the Guerre de Course*. The Hague: Martinus Nijhoff, 1974.

Syrett, David. *Shipping and the American War, 1775–83: A Study of British Transport Organization*. London: Athlone Press, 1970.

Tracy, Nicholas. *Navies, Deterrence, and American Independence: Britain and Seapower in the 1760s and 1770s*. Vancouver, Can.: University of British Columbia Press, 1988.

RELATED CRITICAL STUDIES

Ambrose, Stephen E. *Duty, Honor, Country: A History of West Point*. Baltimore, Md.: Johns Hopkins University Press, 1966.

Baer, George W. *One Hundred Years of Sea Power: The U.S. Navy, 1890–1990*. Stanford, Calif.: Stanford University Press, 1994.

Bassford, Christopher. *Clausewitz in English: The Reception of Clausewitz in Britain and America, 1815–1945*. New York: Oxford University Press, 1994.

Beaumont, Roger. *War, Chaos, and History*. Westport, Conn.: Praeger, 1995.

Berghahn, V. R. *Germany and the Approach of War in 1914*, 2nd ed. New York: St. Martin's, 1993.

Beyerchen, Alan. "Clausewitz, Nonlinearity, and the Unpredictability of War," *International Security* 17 (winter 1992–3): 59–90.

Colby, Charles C. *North Atlantic Arena: Water Transport in the World Order*. Carbondale: Southern Illinois University Press, 1966.

Collins, John M. *Grand Strategy: Principles and Practices*. Annapolis, Md.: Naval Institute Press, 1973.

Cooling, Benjamin Franklin. *Benjamin Franklin Tracy: Father of the Modern American Fighting Navy*. Hamden, Conn.: Archon, 1973.

———. *Gray Steel and Blue Water Navy: The Formative Years of America's Military-Industrial Complex, 1881–1917*. Hamden, Conn.: Archon, 1979.

Corbett, Julian S. "Education in the Navy," *Monthly Review* 6 (March 1902): 34–5.

Dimbleby, David, and David Reynolds. *An Ocean Apart: The Relationship between Britain and America in the Twentieth Century*. New York: Random House, 1988.

Ferris, John, and Michael J. Handel. "Clausewitz, Uncertainty and the Art of Command in Military Operations," *Intelligence and National Security* 10 (January 1995): 1–58.

Gleaves, Rear Admiral Albert. *Life and Letters of Rear Admiral Stephen B. Luce, U.S. Navy, Founder of the Naval War College*. New York: G. P. Putnam's Sons, 1925.

Goldrick, James, and John B. Hattendorf, eds. *Mahan Is Not Enough: The Proceedings of a Conference on the Works of Sir Julian Corbett and Admiral Sir Herbert Richmond*. Newport, R.I.: Naval War College Press, 1993.

Graham, G. S. *The Politics of Naval Supremacy: Studies in British Maritime Ascendancy*. Cambridge, U.K.: Cambridge University Press, 1965.

Hagan, Kenneth J. *This People's Navy: The Making of American Sea Power*. New York: Free Press, 1991.

Hagerman, Edward. "From Jomini to Dennis Hart Mahan," in *Battles Lost and Won*, ed. John T. Hubbell, 31–54. Westport, Conn.: Greenwood, 1975.

Hattendorf, John B., ed. *Doing Naval History: Essays Toward Improvement*. Newport, R.I.: Naval War College Press, 1995.

Hattendorf, John B., B. Mitchell Simpson III, and John R. Wadleigh. *Sailors and Scholars: The Centennial History of the U.S. Naval War College*. Newport, R.I.: Naval War College Press, 1984.

Hayes, John D., and John B. Hattendorf, eds. *The Writings of Stephen B. Luce*. Newport, R.I.: Naval War College Press, 1975.

Herrick, Walter R., Jr. *The American Naval Revolution*. Baton Rouge: Louisiana State University Press, 1966.

Horsfield, John. *The Art of Leadership in War: The Royal Navy from the Age of Nelson to the End of World War II*. Westport, Conn.: Greenwood, 1980.

Howard, Michael. "Jomini and the Classical Tradition in Military Thought," in *The Theory and Practice of War: Essays Presented to Captain B.H. Liddell Hart on his Seventieth Birthday*, ed. Michael Howard, 3–20. New York: Praeger, 1966.

———. *Clausewitz*. New York: Oxford University Press, 1983.

Iriye, Akira. *From Nationalism to Internationalism: U.S. Foreign Policy to 1914*. London: Routledge and Kegan Paul, 1977.

———. *Power and Culture: The Japanese-American War, 1941–1945*. Cambridge, Mass.: Harvard University Press, 1981.

Kennedy, Paul M. *The Rise and Fall of British Naval Mastery*. New York: Charles Scribner's Sons, 1976.

McNeill, William H. *The Pursuit of Power: Technology, Armed Force, and Society since A.D. 1000*. Chicago, Ill.: University of Chicago Press, 1982.

Marder, Arthur J. *The Anatomy of British Sea Power: A History of British Naval Policy in the Pre-Dreadnought Era, 1880–1905*. New York: Alfred A. Knopf, 1940.

Misa, Thomas J. *A Nation of Steel: The Making of Modern America, 1865–1925*. Baltimore, Md.: Johns Hopkins University Press, 1995.

Morrison, James L., Jr. "Military Education and Strategic Thought, 1846–1861," in *Against All Enemies: Interpretations of American Military History from Colonial Times to the Present*, ed. Kenneth J. Hagan and William R. Roberts, 113–31. New York: Greenwood, 1986.

Paret, Peter. *Clausewitz and the State*. Oxford, U.K.: Clarendon, 1976.

———. *Understanding War: Essays on Clausewitz and the History of Military Power.* Princeton, N.J.: Princeton University Press, 1992.

Paret, Peter, and Daniel Moran, ed. and trans. *Carl von Clausewitz: Historical and Political Writings.* Princeton, N.J.: Princeton University Press, 1992.

Preston, Richard A. *Perspectives in the History of Military Education and Professionalism.* Harmon Memorial Lectures in Military History, no. 22. Boulder, Colo.: United States Air Force Academy, 1980.

Pugh, Michael, ed. *Maritime Security and Peacekeeping: A Framework for United Nations Operations.* Manchester, U.K.: Manchester University Press, 1994.

Reynolds, David. *The Creation of the Anglo-American Alliance, 1937–1941: A Study in Competitive Co-operation.* Chapel Hill: University of North Carolina Press, 1982.

Rosenberg, David Alan. "Arleigh Albert Burke," in *The Chiefs of Naval Operation,* ed. Robert William Love, Jr., 262–319. Annapolis, Md.: Naval Institute Press, 1980.

Rosenberg, [David] Alan. "Admiral Arleigh A. Burke," in *Men of War: Great Naval Leaders of World War II,* ed. Stephen Howarth, 506–27. London: Weidenfeld and Nicolson, 1992.

Semmel, Bernard. *Liberalism and Naval Strategy: Ideology, Interest, and Sea Power during the Pax Britannica.* Boston: Allen and Unwin, 1986.

Shulman, Mark R. *Navalism and the Emergence of American Sea Power, 1882–1893.* Annapolis, Md.: Naval Institute Press, 1995.

Shy, John. "Jomini," in *Makers of Modern Strategy from Machiavelli to the Nuclear Age,* ed. Peter Paret, 143–85. Princeton, N.J.: Princeton University Press, 1986.

Simons, William E. *Liberal Education in the Service Academies.* New York: Teachers College, Columbia University Press, 1965.

Spector, Ronald. *Professors of War: The U.S. Naval War College and the Development of the Naval Profession.* Newport, R.I.: Naval War College Press, 1977.

Steele, Ian K. *The English Atlantic, 1675–1740: An Exploration of Communication and Community.* New York: Oxford University Press, 1986.

Sumida, Jon Tetsuro. *In Defence of Naval Supremacy: Finance, Technology and British Naval Policy, 1889–1914.* Boston: Unwin Hyman, 1989.

Todorich, Charles. *The Spirited Years: A History of the Antebellum Naval Academy.* Annapolis, Md.: Naval Institute Press, 1984.

Wallerstein, Immanuel. *The Modern World-System: Capitalist Agriculture and the Origins of the European World-Economy in the Sixteenth Century.* New York: Academic Press, 1976.

MUSIC, ZEN, AND MISCELLANEOUS STUDIES

Barrett, William, ed. *Zen Buddhism: Selected Writings of D. T. Suzuki.* New York: Doubleday Anchor, 1956.

Collingwood, R. G. *The Idea of History.* Oxford, U.K.: Clarendon, 1946.

————. *Essays in the Philosophy of History.* Ed. by William Debbins. New York: McGraw-Hill, 1966.

————. *Essays in Political Philosophy.* Ed. by David Boucher. Oxford, U.K.: Clarendon, 1989.

Dart, Thurston. *The Interpretation of Music.* New York: Harper Colophon, 1963.

Dewey, John. *The Quest for Certainty: A Study of the Relation of Knowledge and Action.* Gifford Lectures 1929. New York: G. P. Putnam's Sons, 1929.

Donagan, Alan. *The Later Philosophy of R. G. Collingwood.* Oxford, U.K.: Clarendon, 1962.

Dray, William H. *History as Re-Enactment: R. G. Collingwood's Idea of History.* Oxford, U.K.: Clarendon, 1995.

Feynman, Richard P. *"Surely You're Joking, Mr. Feynman!": Adventures of a Curious Character.* New York: W. W. Norton, 1985.

Gleick, James. *Chaos: Making of a New Science.* New York: Viking Penguin, 1987.

Gould, Stephen Jay. *Time's Arrow, Time's Cycle: Myth and Metaphor in the Discovery of Geological Time.* Cambridge, Mass.: Harvard University Press, 1987.

————. *Wonderful Life: The Burgess Shale and the Nature of History.* New York: Norton, 1989.

————. *Eight Little Piggies: Reflections in Natural History.* New York: Norton, 1993.

Hammitzsch, Horst. *Zen in the Art of the Tea Ceremony.* New York: Avon, 1982.

Herrigel, Eugen. *The Method of Zen.* Ed. by Hermann Tausend, trans. by R. F. C. Hull. New York: Vintage, 1974.

Kubik, Timothy R.W. "Is Machiavelli's Canon Spiked? Practical Reading in Military History," *Journal of Military History* 61 (January 1997): 7–30.

Locke, John. *An Essay Concerning Human Understanding.* Ed. by A. D. Woozley. Cleveland, Ohio: Meridian, 1964. First published 1690.

McCloskey, Donald M. "History, Differential Equations, and the Problem of Narration," *History and Theory* 30 (1991): 21–36.

Merton, Thomas. *The Way of Chuang Tzu.* New York: New Directions, 1969.

————. *Zen and the Birds of Appetite.* New York: New Directions, 1968.

Miura, Isshu, and Ruth Fuller Sasaki. *The Zen Koan: Its History and Use in Rinzai Zen.* New York: Harcourt Brace, 1965.

O'Brian, Patrick. *Master and Commander.* Philadelphia: J. B. Lippincott, 1969.

Smithers, Don L. "The Baroque Trumpet after 1721: Some Preliminary Observations; Part One: Science and Practice," *Early Music* 5 (April 1977): 177–83.

Sohl, Robert, and Audrey Carr, eds. and comps. *Games Zen Masters Play: Writings of R. H. Blyth.* New York: Mentor, 1976.

Stewart, M. Dee, ed. *Arnold Jacobs: The Legacy of a Master.* Northfield, Ill.: The Instrumentalist, 1987.

Whitehead, Alfred North. "The Aims of Education," in *The Aims of Education and Other Essays,* 1–23. New York: Macmillan, 1959.

Wittgenstein, Ludwig. *Philosophical Investigations.* 3rd ed. Trans. G.E.M. Anscombe. New York: Macmillan, 1958.

Yamada, Koun, ed. *Gateless Gate,* 2nd ed. Tucson: University of Arizona Press, 1990.

Select Analytical Index to
the Writings of Alfred Thayer Mahan

Key to Abbreviations

1812	*Sea Power in Its Relations to the War of 1812*, vol. 1	IntCndtns	*The Interest of America in International Conditions*
1812ii	*Sea Power in Its Relations to the War of 1812*, vol. 2	Intrst	*The Interest of America in Sea Power, Present and Future*
AmRv	*The Major Operations of the Navies in the War of American Independence*	Lssns	*Lessons of the War with Spain and Other Articles*
Arm/Arb	*Armaments and Arbitration*	NgAspcts	*Some Neglected Aspects of War*
Frgt	*Admiral Farragut*		
FrRv	*The Influence of Sea Power upon the French Revolution and Empire, 1793–1812,* vol. 1	Nlsn	*The Life of Nelson*, vol. 1
		Nlsn2	*The Life of Nelson*, vol. 2
		NvAdm	*Naval Administration and Warfare*
FrRv2	*The Influence of Sea Power upon the French Revolution and Empire, 1792–1812,* vol. 2	NvStrtgy	*Naval Strategy*
		PrbAsia	*The Problem of Asia and Its Effect upon International Policies*
Glf	*The Gulf and Inland Waters*	Rtrspct	*Retrospect and Prospect*
Hrvst	*The Harvest Within*	Sl/Stm	*From Sail to Steam*
Infl	*The Influence of Sea Power upon History, 1660–1783*	Types	*Types of Naval Officers Drawn from the History of the British Navy*

AMERICAN SEA POWER

America as an Insular Power

Intrst: 104, 210, 211
Rtrspct: 163–4, 164
NvAdm: 229

American Naval Risk Theory

Intrst: 16, 54–5
Lssns: 286–7, 302, 305
PrbAsia: 182, 183, 186, 189
1812: 321
1812ii: 208–9
NvAdm: 396, 397
IntCndtns: 192
NvStrtgy: 19, 248, 249, 250 (deterrence), 361–2 (inability of European naval powers to commit large naval forces against the United States)

American Resemblance/Nonresemblance to France

Infl: 38, 39, 57–8 (national character), 76, 87
Intrst: 143, 144

American Sea Power

Infl: 26, 29, 33–5, 38, 49 (commercial development), 57–8, 83–4, 84–7, 88, 90–1, 326
FrRv: iv
Frgt: 6, 7
Intrst: 14, 54–5
PrbAsia: 17 (American dependence on Britain), 182
Rtrspct: 8–9, 9, 11, 24, 48, 51, 52–3
NvStrtgy: 331–2
Arm/Arb: 155
AmRv: 4–5

American Sphere of Influence

Rtrspct: 51

Lack of American National Unity

1812ii: 172–3, 436 (defeat as a promoter of national consciousness)

Monroe Doctrine

Infl: 325
Intrst: 150–6
PrbAsia: 16
NvAdm: 374–5, 392, 396, 397–409
IntCndtns: 198–9 (Anglo-German naval balance secures the Monroe Doctrine)
NvStrtgy: 107
Arm/Arb: 39–40, 86

Naval Power and the History of America

Infl: 78–9
FrRv2: 105, 357
Rtrspct: 11
1812: 310–11, 350 (unpreparedness)
1812ii: 318 (unpreparedness)

Open Door

PrbAsia: 163, 167, 201–2
IntCndtns: 181, 192

Panama Canal

Infl: 42, 88
Intrst: 20

Political Subtext in Development of American Navy

Infl: 49, 76, 83–4, 87, 88
FrRv: iv

BRITISH SEA POWER

British Commercial Strength

FrRv: 327
FrRv2: 17, 27, 30, 372–3, 394

British Naval Necessities

Infl: 392, 538
FrRv: 340–1
FrRv2: 74–5
Nlsn: 103 (how to force unwilling foe to fight), 105
Lssns: 48
PrbAsia: 197–8
Rtrspct: 169, 173, 178, 197 (Mediterranean as pivot), 203–5 (imperial defense)
1812: 86–7
IntCndtns: 59–66, 66, 111–113, 114, 118 (formal alliance not needed), 160
NvStrtgy: 82, 371
Arm/Arb: 27

British Naval Supremacy in the Eighteenth and Nineteenth Centuries

Infl: 225, 328–9
NgAspcts: 168 (unlikely to be replicated)

British Vulnerability

Infl: 340 (defensive grand strategy), 392, 538
1812ii: 209 (difficulty in restraining Napoleonic sea power)

Relative Decline of Britain

Infl: 67 (unwillingness to support naval power)
Intrst: 130
Rtrspct: 245
IntCndtns: 142–3, 149–50, 151–2, 163 (budgetary difficulties, social decadence, and lack of discipline)

NvStrtgy: 73, 110, 371
Arm/Arb: 20, 60–61

Strategy of Attrition

FrRv2: 199–200, 406, 409, 411
Nlsn: 105

Two-Power Standard

Infl: 523
Types: 144
Arm/Arb: 62

COMMAND

Creation of Naval Staff

NvAdm: 48

Group Decision-Making

FrRv: 305
Nlsn2: 136–7
NvStrtgy: 19–20

Making Mistakes

Lssns: 169
NvStrtgy: 384, 430–1

Naval Professional Character

Glf: 16, 45, 84n
Infl: 126–9, 332–3 (egalitarianism as a source of corruption)
FrRv: 38, 40–1, 102
FrRv2: 141
Frgt: 35, 44–5, 54, 69–70, 107 (strength of character), 113, 150, 159,
201 (readiness to act but no precipitation), 216 (stern resolution), 232

(judgment), 239–40 (tactical genius), 269–70, 309–10, 312, 314–5, 317–8, 319, 324–5, 325
Nlsn: 190–1, 224
Types: 100, 151, 186, 256–7, 340 (power and responsibilities of naval executive rank), 341 (professional self-respect), 389, 459
Rtrspct: 290
1812: 354
1812ii: 154–5, 241–2
Sl/Stm: 46

On Calculation

Glf: 227–8, 232–3
Nlsn2: 302–3, 305

On Opportunity

Glf: 86 (value of promptness in war), 101–2
Nlsn: 226, 264 (fleeting and may never occur), 358

Patronage

Nlsn2: 240–1

Subdivided Fleet Command

Infl: 112, 112–3

Taking Risks

Glf: 34–5, 36, 235, 239
Infl: 396, 476, 478
FrRv: 226
Frgt: 31, 142, 143–4, 223 (timid precaution may entail the greatest of risks), 269–70, 309, 309–10
Nlsn: 125 (quest for certainty great snare of the mere engineer), 196 (Nelsonian miscalculation), 196–7, 182 (high cost of missing opportunities), 320, 322, 326, 336, 358
Nlsn2: 138, 280, 305, 344
Lssns: 23, 190

Types: 84, 142
Rtrspct: 189, 193
1812ii: 99
Hrvst: 24, 253–4 (emotion)
NvStrtgy: 430–1
AmRv: 104, 174

Willingness to Assume Responsibility

Infl: 381
FrRv: 205, 229, 371
Frgt: 183, 317–8, 318
Nlsn: 84, 112, 113, 125, 189, 190, 190–1 (on disobedience), 283 (on disobedience), 297, 312 (necessity of mental and moral power), 452–3
Nlsn2: 291, 302–3, 306 (man of faith a man of works), 324
Types: 130, 142
Rtrspct: 264–5, 270, 273, 279–83
Hrvst: 7

HISTORICAL TECHNIQUE

Acceptance of Contrary Truths

PrbAsia: 1
NvStrtgy: 386–7

Criticism of Academic History

Sl/Stm: 86

Dangers of Reasoning by Analogy

Infl: 2–3, 5, 89
NvStrtgy: 44–5 (favorable to analogies)

Difficulty of Writing about Recent Events

Lssns: 21–2, 22–3, 24
PrbAsia: vi–vii

Lssns: 24 (impossibility of certainty of knowledge without unacceptable delay)
Rtrspct: 190 (disturbing political possibilities must be reasonably viewed)

Historical Sophistication—Evidence Issues

Glf: v
Infl: 250, 442
FrRv: 273
Nlsn: 86
1812ii: 20–1, 88, 96

History as Experience

Hrvst: vi–vii, 272, 273–4
NvStrtgy, 9–10, 297–8

Jomini, Criticism of

Nlsn: 235

Lessons of History

Infl: 2, 11, 83–4, 89
FrRv: 119, 201
Types: vii
1812: v, 327
1812ii: 208
PrbAsia: vi
Sl/Stm: 282
NvAdm: 167, 229
NvStrtgy: 115, 383
AmRv: v, 4

Principles

Infl: 7 (as distinguished from precedent), 9, 10, 88, 478
Lssns: 6–7, 10, 11, 168–9 (acting contrary to the weight of experience), 170
1812: 319 (need for intelligent application of), 327

1812ii: 54 (details vs. principles), 82 (importance of circumstances), 83 (exception)
Sl/Stm: 82, 282 (principles as opposed to pedantic precedents), 283
NvAdm: x, 95 (principle as a generalization), 191 (on difficulties of application), 366
Hrvst: 269 (impracticability of generalities)
NvStrtgy: 2, 10, 17, 18, 44–5, 49, 61–2, 74–5 (upholding principles in spirit), 112, 115, 118, 119, 120–1 (law facilitates judgment), 234 (difficulty of applying principles as in the case of morals), 240, 297 (sound application of principles a matter of experience), 300 (maxims of war not positive rules but application of principles), 318, 390–1, 429 (circumstances alter cases)
Arm/Arb: 68 (difficulty of application)

Shortcomings of Experience Based on Faulty Thinking

Types: 16–7, 19
Sl/Stm: 40, 41
NvAdm: 194
NvStrtgy: 11–12

Writing Style

Sl/Stm: 288, 288–9, 291

HISTORY

Contempt for History

Infl: 11
FrRv: v
Sl/Stm: 40
NvAdm: 232–3
NvStrtgy: 11–12

Determinative Conditions that Shape History

PrbAsia: v–vi

Difficulty of Analyzing Recent Events

Lssns: 21–2

God, Role of

Intrst: 243, 307
PrbAsia: 175
NgAspcts: 103–4

Gossip the Truest History

Sl/Stm: vi, vi–vii

Influence of Mahan's Historical Writing on Events

PrbAsia: v
Sl/Stm: 325–6
NvStrtgy: 112

Influence of Sea Power upon History

Infl: iii, v–vi, 1, 102

Poverty of Past Naval History

Sl/Stm: 279

Qualification of Influence of Sea Power upon History

Infl: iii, v–vi, 1, 21 (disclaims exclusive influence), 90–1, 102, 225–6

Relevance of History

Lssns: 4–5, 12, 13, 14 (as preceptor of mass electorates)
NvAdm: vii, 94, 191–2, 223–9, 251–2
Hrvst: v
NvStrtgy: 115, 299, 383 (lessons of history)

Steam Warfare Has No History

Infl: 2
NvStrtgy: 115

Study of History and Enhancement of Military Performance

Infl: 1–2, 11
Nlsn: 103, 208 (trained vs. untrained intelligence), 234, 235
Lssns: 4–5
Sl/Stm: 41

Tendency of General Historians to Ignore Naval History

Infl: iii
FrRv: 150n
Lssns: 277 (sea an unfamiliar place for mass of mankind), 279
Sl/Stm: 276

MISCELLANEOUS

Abolition of Slavery

Sl/Stm: 91–2, 92

Danger of Engineering Mindsets

Lssns: 25

Danger of Overestimating Your Enemy

1812: 65

Danger of Underestimating Your Enemy

Lssns: 31

Embargo

1812: 186

Guerrilla War

Rtrspct: 63, 74, 75, 76

Friction

Nlsn2: 129

Importance of Geography

PrbAsia: v
NvStrtgy: 132, 134–5, 135–6, 139

Mediterranean as a Strategic Problem

Rtrspct: 180–5, 197

Origins of Line of Battle

Infl: 115

Origins of Term "Battleship"

Lssns: 261–2

Prestige

Rtrspct: 57–8, 58

Too Much Success

Nlsn: 296

Weather

Infl: 300–2, 458, 518–9, 527
FrRv: 164, 219, 256, 343–4
Nlsn: 225
Nlsn2: 24, 269, 278
1812ii: 192
AmRv: 98, 159

Wind

Infl: 362
FrRv: 114, 159–60, 164, 165, 345, 349
FrRv2: 151
Frgt: 38
Nlsn: 225
Nlsn2: 24, 278

Women's Suffrage (Opposition to)

Sl/Stm: 150

NAVAL ADMINISTRATION

Administration/Policy Organization

NvAdm: 58, 69, 71 (only corporate life endures), 73, 84, 85
Arm/Arb: 75–7

Importance of Naval Administration and Logistics

Glf: 91
Infl: 442, 443, 451, 477–8, 514
FrRv: 184, 371
FrRv2: 122
Frgt: 69, 239, 249 (drudgery of)
Nlsn: 250, 320
Nlsn2: 171–2, 197, 197–200, 207–9, 215, 244, 314, 329
Lssns: 41 (distance between coaling stations), 175 (on coal)
Types: 108–9, 122, 130 (administrative details of interest only to specialists), 336
Rtrspct: 42–4
1812: 284 (on coal), 372 (secure communications)
Sl/Stm: 177
NvAdm: 6–7, 7–8, 8–9, 9–10, 10, 51, 69, 71, 206, 206–7, 317 (on training), 320, 321, 322–3, 336, 340–1, 342, 353

NvStrtgy: 118–119 (advent of steam, logistics more important), 163 (vital importance of dry docks), 381 (steam has imposed fetters on strategic deployment of fleets)
Arm/Arb: 196, 200–201

Manpower

Glf: 104
Infl: 536–7
FrRv: 102
FrRv2: 141
Nlsn: 224, 451 (do not waste trained seamen in amphibious operations)
Nsln2: 132, 207–9
Intrst: 202–3, 203, 205 (trained men, more than ships and guns, the basis of preparedness), 213–4
Lssns: 314 (importance of having sufficient numbers of trained personnel)
PrbAsia: 199–200 (importance of trained men)
1812: 15 (shipping and manpower)
1812ii: 63, 64–5 (on race and ability)
NvStrtgy: 446–7

Naval Bases

Infl: 443
FrRv: 184
Rtrspct: 42 (as basis for offensive action), 44–7, 47, 154–5, 159 (bases as force multipliers)
1812ii: 59, 118
NvAdm: 128
NvStrtgy: 76, 163, 249, 434–5

Naval Finance

Glf: 14, 16
Infl: 169–70, 195 (inadequacy of state finance as the reason for privateering by governments), 227, 227–8
FrRv: 4, 96

FrRv2: 107, 111, 338 (Napoleonic France could not inspire fiscal confidence), 339 (British financial advantage—ability to borrow), 340
Nlsn2: 62
1812: 317 (difficulty of making ends meet when there is not enough to go around)
NvAdm: 142, 142–3
NvStrtgy: 446–7
Arm/Arb: 17, 18, 33–5, 59–60, 60–61

Retrenchment

NvAdm: 78

NAVAL THEORY

Doctrine

Arm/Arb: 202, 204, 206
NvStrtgy: 201, 204

Strategy

Infl: 8–9, 9, 11, 88, 89
Frgt: 171–2, 237, 238, 311
1812ii: 124 (reasons for flank attacks)
Types: 269–70 (strategy a more creative field than tactics)
Rtrspct: 162–4 (need of insular states for offensive strategy)
NvAdm: 206
NvStrtgy: 2, 250–1 (principle of strategy—command of controlling point or system of points), 417, 421

Tactics

Infl: 10, 88, 506–7
Types: 12 (line of battle), 15, 16–17

POLITICS AND WAR, NATURE OF

Anti-war Tendency of Commercial Culture

Rtrspct: 143–4, 145 (warlike tendency as well)

Communications

PrbAsia: 125 (dominant factor in war)

Democracy

NgAspcts: x, xx
Arm/Arb: 59–60, 74–5

Democratic Countries' Need for Sufficient Organized Force

Infl: 48–9, 82

Desirability of Having Sufficient Force from the Start

Glf: 7, 16
AmRv: 29

Deterrence

Intrst: 171–2
Lssns: 286–7, 302 (defense is not primarily the power to protect but the power to injure)
1812: vii–viii, 229
1812ii: 208–9

Inspiration of Fear in Enemy

1812: 298

Legitimacy of Use of Power and Force

PrbAsia: 142
NgAspcts: 47, 64, 72, 93
Sl/Stm: 324

Localism and Government

IntCndtns: 3, 4, 6, 6–7

Military Operations and Public Opinion in a Democracy

Rtrspct: 68, 69

Modern War Short and a Matter of Striking a Quick Blow

Infl: 46

Need in Democratic Countries for Military Interest to Be Supported by Strongly Represented Interest

Infl: 88

Political Economy of Quick Victory

Glf: 86
Infl: 416
1812ii: 95

Political vs. Military Considerations

Rtrspct: 140, 142, 143
Sl/Stm: 283 (war is not fighting but business; attribution to Jomini)

Sentiment in the Affairs of Nations

Sl/Stm: 86
Arm/Arb: 126

Slowness of Men to Respond to Changing Conditions

Infl: 10
Types: 16–7
Rtrspct: 8–9, 9
1812: 44–5

Tendency of Exchanges to Escalate

1812ii: 335

Time Needed to Prepare for War under Modern Conditions

Intrst: 176, 202–3

Unwillingness of Democratic Countries to Spend on Defense

Infl: 67, 88
Intrst: 175 (extensive and complicated preparation for war in modern times exceeds capacities of national treasury)
Lssns: 20
1812: 262, 281–2 (economy vs. preparation), 310–11, 350
1812ii: 27, 318

OPERATIONS

Battle Fleets as the Only Determining Factor in Naval War

Nlsn2: 196
Lssns: 262, 272–3
Rtrspct: 168, 194–5
1812ii: 59 (exception—ports not fleet), 229

Blockade

Glf: 4
Infl: 525, 526, 527
FrRv: 99
FrRv2: 118
Nlsn2: 269
Lssns: 106
Types: 108–9
Rtrspct: 176, 179–80, 194
1812: 286–7, 288
1812ii: 14
NgAspcts: 173–4

Characteristics of Defense

NvStrtgy: 277, 279–80, 293

Coastal Defense

Infl: 453

FrRv: 321, 341–2
Nlsn2: 121–2, 131
Lssns: xii–xiii, 48–50, 63–9
Rtrspct: 205–6 (imperial defense)
1812: 299 (use of fleet by weaker power), 321, 326
1812ii: 150–1, 154–5, 159, 160 (unfruitful record of gunboats all over world)
NvStrtgy: 147, 249, 293 (when country is on the defensive with regard to shoreline, best course to take the offensive), 433–4

Combined Operations

Frgt: 199–200, 206, 217, 232, 244, 290–1
FrRv: 208
FrRv2: 252
Nlsn: 208, 213, 227, 451 (do not risk trained seamen in amphibious operations)
NvStrtgy: 189, 190, 243

Commerce Destruction or Protection

Infl: 8–9, 31, 132–8, 138 (clear statement of Mahan's complex position on the subject), 148–9, 179 (general inadequacy of commerce-raiding when not supported by fleets), 195, 196 (commerce-raiding unsupported by battle fleets will only result in the loss of cruisers), 229–30, 400, 539–40 (commerce-raiding as the basis of national naval defense a dangerous delusion when presented in the fascinating garb of cheapness), 540n
FrRv: 179, 180 (battle fleet as the central mass and thus the necessary underpinning of cruiser warfare), 203, 328
FrRv2: 197, 199, 218
Frgt: 18–9, 19
Intrst: 128, 128–9 (protection and destruction of trade the purpose of navies), 133, 133–4
Lssns: 71–4
Rtrspct: 194–5 (battle fleet as basis of cruiser control)
1812: 286 (sea militia), 286–7, 288 (weapon of weaker power), 327
1812ii: 126 (cruiser warfare secondary and not determinative of great issues on its own; note hint of qualification), 127, 222, 229
NgAspcts: 193
NvAdm: 162

Concentration of Force

Infl: 414
FrRv: 180, 201·
FrRv2: 157–8
Nlsn2: 129
Lssns: 43, 110–11 (concentration of purpose as well as force), 258–9 (achieved by numbers *and* mobility)
Types: 408–9
1812: v, 315–6, 319
1812ii: 97, 101, 272–3
NvAdm: 167, 168–9, 172–3
NvStrtgy: 4–5, 5–6, 39, 43, 44, 58, 61–2, 69, 73, 74–5, 75, 93–4, 125, 271, 273
Arm/Arb: 201

Contingency

Infl: 471, 484
FrRv: v, 219, 335–6, 349
FrRv2: 151, 152, 182 (complexity of sea warfare makes accurate assessment of chances of success difficult), 201 (when forces closely balanced, prediction of outcomes impossible)
Nlsn: 163 (good luck), 165, 358 (luck as something that can be sought)
Nlsn2: 269, 278, 344
1812: 396 (need for careful preparation as well as reliance on chance)
1812ii: 398

Convoy

Nlsn2: 243
1812: 409 (independently routed ships much easier to detect than those concentrated in convoy)
1812ii: 130, 216

Effects of Numerical Superiority

FrRv: 276
Nlsn2: 130, 217
Types: 15–6, 408–9
1812ii: 101

Enemy Battle Fleet as the Main Object

FrRv: 328
Nlsn: 171
Nlsn2: 196, 271
Lssns: 139
Rtrspct: 168
1812ii: 59 (exception to the rule), 118, 132

Field Fortification and the Resilience of Militia

Types: vii

Fleet in Being

Nlsn: 136–7, 196–7
Lssns: 75–84
NvAdm: 149–52, 152
NvStrtgy: 428

Fleet Formation Discipline

Infl: 465
FrRv: 38, 40–1
Types: 291–2 (necessity of fleet drill), 309, 388–9
1812ii: 139 (fleet disorder as prerequisite to defeat)

Flotilla

Infl: 113
Nlsn: 192, 224
Nlsn2: 122, 131, 132
Intrst: 196–7
Lssns: 147
NvAdm: 111–113, 113, 120–1 (Japanese should depend on torpedo vessels and army rather than the fleet)
NvStrtgy: 147, 148

Forcing an Unwilling Foe to Fight

Nlsn: 103, 105

Intelligence/Command and Control

Infl: 112 (divisional tactics), 112–3, 521
FrRv2: 157–8
Nlsn: 234
Nlsn2: 299 (misled by false intelligence), 364 (difficulty of controlling large fleets)
Lssns: 140–1, 142

Offensive Action

Glf: 4
Infl: 394, 426
FrRv: 199, 201, 340–1
Nlsn: 176, 319
Lssns: 163–4, 286–7
Types: 15, 19
Rtrspct: 40, 42, 151–2, 152–3, 153, 154, 155–6, 163–4 (need of insular states for offensive strategy), 168 (fundamental principle of all naval war: defense insured only by offense), 193
1812: 298, 326
1812ii: 99
NgAspcts: 191
NvStrtgy: 243, 248, 250–1, 274

Particular Operations vs. Destruction of Enemy Forces

Infl: 338–9, 425, 478, 482, 538
FrRv: 335–6
Nlsn: 176

Purpose of Battles

NvAdm: 120, 120–1, 121–2
NvStrtgy: 220 (purpose and value of diversionary attack)

Signaling

Nlsn2: 345
Types: 82

Value of a Battle Even When Lost

Nlsn2: 323
AmRv: 18, 25, 27

OTHER NAVAL POWERS

French Sea Power

Infl: 53, 53–4, 70, 72–3, 74, 76, 103, 170, 179, 197–8, 226, 425
FrRv: 4, 96
FrRv2: 107
Rtrspct: 247

German Militarism and Naval Threat

Intrst: 8
Lssns: 289–98
Rtrspct: 191, 245–6, 247, 248
IntCndtns: 32–40, 40, 42–3, 46–7, 49–59, 68, 81–2, 95–102, 103–111, 163, 170–1, 172–3, 194–6
NvStrtgy: 105–6, 108, 110, 363, 369, 371
Arm/Arb: 17, 29, 57–8

Russian Aggressiveness

PrbAsia: 44, 63
Rtrspct: 250–1

PERSONS

Bonaparte, Napoleon

FrRv: 290, 305, 326
FrRv2: 25, 27, 74, 98, 171, 197, 199–200, 279 (water and wizards), 338, 407
Nlsn2: 271
Lssns: 305
Hrvst: vii, 259

Corbett, Julian

NgAspcts: 115–54 (author of chapter)
NvStrtgy: 26–7

Darwin, Charles

Sl/Stm: 285

Decatur, Stephen

Sl/Stm: 39

Jomini, Antoine-Henri

Infl: 21
Nlsn: 235 (genius combined with good education)
Sl/Stm: 278, 283 (what Mahan learned from Jomini)
NvStrtgy: 4,17, 46, 51, 107, 127, 241, 255, 267, 299, 130, 149, 282, 300, 394, 402

Lawrence, James

1812ii: 145

Macaulay, Thomas Babbington

FrRv2: 394

Madison, James

1812: 106

Pitt, William (Younger)

FrRv: 5
FrRv2: 74–5, 108, 364, 366, 391 (revealing anecdote), 411

St. Vincent, Lord (Sir John Jervis)

FrRv: 204, 205, 206, 229, 310, 374
FrRv2: 122

Smith, Adam

1812: 1

Suffren, Pierre-Andre de

Infl: 425, 426, 443, 465

Washington, George

Infl: 400 (on necessity of sea power)

SEA AND NAVAL POWER

Economy of Water Transport

Infl: 25–6
PrbAsia: 38, 125–6
1812ii: 17–9
NgAspcts: 176–7

Effects of Naval Supremacy

Infl: 400, 416
FrRv: 325
FrRv2: 202–3, 372–3 (sea power defined), 374–5, 386, 400–1
Nlsn: 97 (Moscow and Waterloo as inevitable consequences of Trafalgar)
Nlsn2: 397–8
Intrst: 125
1812ii: 35
Sl/Stm: 4
NvStrtgy: 139, 256, 260–1 (not absolute)
Arm/Arb: 122, 132

Factors Advertent and Inadvertent Influencing Growth of Sea Power

Infl: 28, 66–74
FrRv2: 372–3 (sea power defined)

Rtrspct: 48 (events political, economic, and commercial as the force driving naval expansion in the late nineteenth century)
NvStrtgy: 446–7
Arm/Arb: 161 (demography, economics, political culture)

Finance and Power

Infl: 169–70, 227, 227–8
FrRv2: 100, 107, 108, 111, 199–200, 337–8, 339, 340, 386
1812: 284–5, 291–2, 296
NvAdm: 162
IntCndtns: 208
NvStrtgy: 371
Arm/Arb: 122

National Reserves

Infl: 46, 48, 48–9
Intrst: 206–7

Navies as Complex Institutions

FrRv: 36–7, 39, 39–40

Navies as a Deterrent

Frgt: 7
Intrst: 171–2
Lssns: 286–7, 305
1812ii: 208–9
NvStrtgy: 78
Arm/Arb: 16–17

Navies as Organized Force

Infl: 112, 325, 326, 373, 416, 465, 538
Lssns: 251
PrbAsia: 191
Types: 291–2
Rtrspct: 40, 168 (equation of battle fleet and organized force)

1812ii: 118, 120, 132 (organized force the prime object of all military effort)
Sl/Stm: 29 (essence of battleship combined action), 283 (attribution to Jomini of principle of organized force as the prime object of all military effort), 324
NvStrtgy: 176, 254, 260

Navies as Political Factors

FrRv: 229
Frgt: 7
PrbAsia: 35–40 (sea power in relation to land power), 51–2
Sl/Stm: 283
NvAdm: 120, 121–2
NvStrtgy: 21

Sea Power as a Better Investment than Land Power

Infl: 75, 103, 170, 225–6 (sea power as the central link in the acquisition of national wealth), 253, 328–9, 400
PrbAsia: 38, 39–40, 51–2

TECHNOLOGY

Personnel, Greater Importance of

FrRv: 102
FrRv2: 141
Frgt: 324
Types: 300
1812ii: 52
Sl/Stm: 25

Warship Design

FrRv: 38, 128 (big ship superior to several smaller vessels of equal aggregate tonnage)
Lssns: 37 (size vs. numbers), 38–9, 39–42, 151 (importance of unity of conception), 152, 257 (design of warships a military not a technical

question), 260, 261, 261–2, 264–5, 266, 267–9, 269, 270–1 (on armored cruisers), 310 (quick-firing guns not big guns are the primary armament), 318 (agreement with Ruskin observation about battleships)
Types: 19
Rtrspct: 176 (armored cruisers and blockade)
1812: 43 (larger ships are better gun platforms than smaller)
1812ii: 97, 150–1, 154–5
Sl/Stm: 23, 30, 35
NvAdm: 20 (money and design), 141, 154–5
NvStrtgy: 44, 390–1
Arm/Arb: 18–19 (battle cruisers)

Wireless

NvStrtgy: 318, 330–331, 343

TRADE AND RELATED MATTERS

Colonies

Rtrspct: 112–3, 113–5, 125, 131

Communications

Intrst: 282
PrbAsia: 125, 197–8
1812: 372
NgAspcts: 179 (dependence of modern societies on international economy)
NvStrtgy: 26–7 (mentions Corbett), 68, 99, 139, 166 (communications dominate war), 176, 178, 190, 303

Economics and State Power: Necessity of External Trade

Infl: 53,198, 200, 209, 227, 243 (favor of free trade)
FrRv2: 27, 30, 107, 108, 197, 409 (economy, not military forces, the target of strategy when opponent a truly great power), 411 (Britain shut Napoleon off from world and thus prolonged her own powers of endurance beyond his power of aggression)

Nlsn2: 62
Intrst: 4–5 (favors free trade)
Rtrspct: 143, 143–4 (effect of free trade), 145, 149 (commerce as the primary focus of external policy of states)
1812: 15, 144, 284–5 (clear statement of the relationship between sea commerce and national credit), 296 (commerce and finance), 400
NgAspcts: 173
Arm/Arb: 132

Relationship of Production, Shipping, and Colonies

Infl: 28
1812: 57

Trade and Navies

Infl: 26, 49
Rtrspct: 143, 143–4, 144–5, 149
NvStrtgy: 302, 303, 445–6 (qualifies former insistence that a necessary connection exists between maritime commercial and naval development)

Trade and Trade Routes

Infl: 25
PrbAsia: 38 (costs of land vs. sea transport)
NvStrtgy: 68, 139

WORLD POLITICS

Anglo-American Relations

Intrst: 27, 55, 84–5, 107, 108, 10, 111, 112, 113, 185, 188, 257
Lssns: viii
PrbAsia: 17, 109, 123, 133, 138 (large part of nation's wisdom to be found in cooperation with others), 145 (Anglo-American cooperation based upon common language), 177–8, 180, 186, 187, 187–8, 195–6, 197–8
Rtrspct: 34, 134–5
IntCndtns: 75–6, 76–8, 80, 81–2, 161

NvStrtgy: 107, 331–332
Arm/Arb: 29, 30, 180 (coincidence of American and British interests; navy second to that of Britain), 194 (navy second to none but Britain)

Anglo-German Relations

Rtrspct: 247, 248, 249, 249–50, 250–1

Arbitration

NgAspcts: vii–viii

Asian Threat, Development of

Intrst: 123–4, 234–7
PrbAsia: 73–4, 77, 90–1, 95, 101, 148, 148–9
Rtrspct: 14–16, 34–5 (importance of Shanghai and the possibility of a Shanghai-based government strong enough to challenge Peking)
IntCndtns: 130–1, 138
Arm/Arb: 142–3

Competition between Europeans as a Progressive Force

PrbAsia: 26, 94–5, 95
Sl/Stm: 10
Arm/Arb: 120

Expediency

Frgt: 7
1812: 8
Arm/Arb: 243, 249

Future Development of World Politics

Infl: 325
PrbAsia: v, 17, 26 (world federation)
Rtrspct: 150
IntCndtns: 202–4
Arm/Arb: 8–10, 13

Future World Conflicts

Infl: 325
Intrst: 122
PrbAsia: v, 46 (concern not with balance of power in particular sense but character of systemic equilibrium), 63 (community of interest between Germany, Great Britain, Japan, and United States against Russia), 99–100, 157–8
Types: ix (America as mediator)
Rtrspct: 50, 52–3, 150 (Pacific, not Atlantic), 246 (war increasingly unnatural)
IntCndtns: 121–4, 161, 163, 166
NvStrtgy: 363
Arm/Arb: 110–111, 116, 142–3

God, Role of

Intrst: 243, 307
PrbAsia: 175
NgAspcts: 103–4

Immigration and Territorial Claims

Infl: 283
Intrst: 226
Arm/Arb: 8, 161, 163, 178–9

Imperialism

Rtrspct: 18 (Mahan's conversion from anti-imperialist into imperialist), 110 (imperialism not a particular form of government), 111

Modern War as Business not Fighting

Arm/Arb: 64

National Self-interest

PrbAsia: 97
1812: vii (need for force)
Arm/Arb: 124, 28

Naval Arms Races

1812ii: 52, 95

Obligation to Defend Right in International Relations

1812: viii
1812ii: 334
NgAspcts: 47

Race Questions

PrbAsia: v, 95, 111–18
NvAdm: 346, 349, 351, 352–3

Rights of Indigenous Populations

PrbAsia: 73–4, 97–8, 98–9, 171 (we meddle not with China's national affairs until they become internationally unendurable)

Tendency of Wars to Spread

AmRv: 1

Transnational Cooperation

PrbAsia: 57–8, 63 (interests of Germany, Britain, Japan, and United States related and against those of Russia), 104, 108, 109, 123, 133, 145 (Anglo-American cooperation based upon common language), 177–8 (limits of national strength and the necessity of cooperation), 181 (international conditions impose mutual support), 248, 249
NgAspcts: 179, 181 (transnational interest in international trade)

Unpreparedness

Glf: 14, 16
Frgt: 16, 115–6, 242
1812: 281–2, 291, 291–2, 310–11, 350
1812ii: 27, 318

Index

Admiral Farragut, 57–61

American Revolutionary War, 30–2, 49;
 Britain in, 43–4; France in, 55

art and art of war, xii–xiv, xvii, 5, 12–13,
 21, 61, 65, 70, 100, 103–5, 110, 112, 117

Ashe, Samuel A., 15–16, 22

Asia: military threat of, 93–7, 108–9

battle, 24, 35, 37–9, 43–4, 75–6, 101–2;
 limitations of, 34, 44, 75–6

blockade. *See* commerce-raiding

Bridge, Captain A. G., 61

Britain: in American Revolutionary War,
 30–2; financial support for navy of,
 84–7; in *The Influence of Sea Power upon
 the French Revolution and Empire,
 1792–1812*, 33–6; naval strategy of,
 43–4; naval supremacy of, 4, 27–9,
 101; new ships of, 24–5, 63–4; relative
 decline of, 84–6; transnational cooperation of, 88–92, 95, 107–9

Burke, Arleigh, 114–15

Castex, Raoul, 3

Civil War, 19–21, 57–61

Clausewitz, Carl von, xi, 7, 9, 73, 110–14

commerce-raiding, 19–20, 33–4, 45–8, 72

experience, xiii, 69, 79, 99, 104–5, 113,
 115

Farragut, David Glasgow, 19–21; biography of, 57–61

Feynman, Richard, 42

Foote, Andrew Hall, 20

France: administration of navy of, 29–32,
 55–6, 64–5; in American Revolutionary
 War, 49, 55; British commerce-raiding
 of, 33–4; naval potential of, 29–32, 101;
 navy of, 32–6

Gould, Stephen Jay, 1, 26

governmental argument, 107–9; and
 authoritarian rule, 29–30, 87; defined,
 6; and democracy, 66–7, 84–8, 102–3;
 in "Influence of Sea Power" series,
 30–1, 34–5, 40–1, 100–1; Mahan's
 reversal of, 81

*Harvest Within, The: Thoughts on the Life
 of a Christian*, 76–9

Henderson, W. H., 24

"Influence of Sea Power" series. *See Influence of Sea Power upon History,
 1660–1783, The; Influence of Sea Power
 upon the French Revolution and Empire,
 1793–1812, The; Life of Nelson, The: The
 Embodiment of the Sea Power of Great
 Britain; Sea Power in Its Relations to the
 War of 1812*

Influence of Sea Power upon History,
   1660–1783, The: American Revolutionary War in, 31–2, 49; arguments in, 4,
   26–8, 30–2; Britain in, 4, 28–9, 43–4;
   criticism of, 3, 33; France in, 29–31;
   popularity of, 1–2; published, 24–5;
   strategy in, 42–3, 45–8
*Influence of Sea Power upon the French
   Revolution and Empire, 1793–1812, The,*
   32–6; strategy in, 48
*Interest of America in Sea Power, Present and
   Future, The,* 61–3; naval administration
   in, 64–7; naval architecture in, 63–4
intuition, xvi, 17, 104

Jervis, Sir John (Lord St. Vincent), 53
Jomini, Antoine-Henri, 4, 23–4, 43,
   109–10

Kennedy, Paul, 1

Lawrence, James, 51–2
leadership, 16–17, 36–9, 48–9, 51–4,
   58–61, 116–17; in the Civil War, 20–1;
   defined, 5–6; elements of, 56, 64–7; and
   strategy, 69–71. *See also* naval professional argument
*Life of Nelson, The: The Embodiment of the
   Sea Power of Great Britain,* 36–9
Louis XIV: navy under, 29–31
Luce, Stephen, 22, 23, 25

Mahan, Alfred Thayer: arguments of,
   5–7, 40, 80–1, 100–1, 105–7; as author,
   1–3; autobiography of, 64, 71–2; correspondence of, 15–16, 22, 24, 39, 61, 90;
   critical analysis of, 3–5, 7–8, 114–16;
   criticism of U.S. Navy by, 15–16, 40–1,
   54–5, 60; on education of officers,
   16–19, 21–3, 104–5; influence of
   Clausewitz on, 73, 110–14; influence of
   Dennis Hart Mahan on, 13–14; influence of Jomini on, 4, 23–4, 43, 109–10;
   influence of Mommsen on, 22–3; naval
   career of, 14–16, 21–4; and religion, 4,
   76–9, 98; retirement of, 2, 40, 61; role
   of, 99–100; on transnational cooperation, 82–4, 92–7
Mahan, Dennis Hart, 7, 9–14, 109–14
McIntyre, James W., 90
Mommsen, Theodor, 22–3
Mumonkan, xi, 57, 99

Napoleon, 34, 65
naval professional argument, 103–4; in
   Admiral Farragut, 58–61; defined, 6; in

"Influence of Sea Power" series, 48–9,
   51–3; in *The Interest of America in Sea
   Power, Present and Future,* 62–7; and officers, 54–6. *See also* leadership
Nelson, Horatio, 43–5; leadership of,
   36–9, 49, 59–60; quoted, 51, 53

O'Brian, Patrick, xivn2, 42

Pitt, William, 34
political argument, 103, 107–9; defined, 6;
   in "Influence of Sea Power" series, 27,
   30–1, 33–6, 40
political-economic argument, 92–4, 103;
   defined, 6–7; in "Influence of Sea
   Power" series, 27–8, 30–2, 34–6; reversal of, 40, 80–2

Rhodes, James Ford, 39
Russo-Japanese War, 63–4, 75, 80–1

*Scribner's Magazine, Sea Power in Its Rela-
   tions to the War of 1812* in, 40
*Sea Power in Its Relations to the War of
   1812,* 51–2; arguments in, 40–1; in
   Scribner's Magazine, 40; strategy in, 44,
   46–8
Spain, 35, 49
strategy, 5–7, 67, 72–3, 101–4; amphibious operations as, 45; of Britain, 43–4;
   coastal defense as, 48, 73; commerce-
   raiding as, 45–8; concentration of force
   as, 76; contradictions by Mahan of,
   105–7; defined, 5–6; effects on, 50–1;
   elements of, 68–71, 74
Suffren, Pierre-André de, 32, 49
Suzuki, D. T., vi, 59

Trafalgar, 35, 37–9, 44
transnational cooperation, 88–92, 95, 102;
   Anglo-American, 93–4, 107–9

United States: building of navy by, 30,
   82–4; transnational cooperation of,
   88–95, 107–9
U.S. Navy: criticism of, 15–16, 40–1,
   54–5, 60–1

Wallerstein, Immanuel, 80
War of 1812. *See Sea Power in Its Relations
   to the War of 1812*
Wittgenstein, Ludwig, 99, 116n30

Zenrin Kushu, 9, 80